THE MESSAGE of the NEW TESTAMENT

THE REVELATION - I

by FRANK PACK

Published by
BIBLICAL RESEARCH PRESS
1334 Ruswood Drive
Abilene, Texas
79601

THE MESSAGE OF
THE NEW TESTAMENT

THE REVELATION - I
by Frank Pack

Library of Congress Catalog Card No. 83-073011
ISBN 0-89112-176-5

FOREWORD

The author is grateful to the many readers who have expressed in various ways their appreciation of this work. First published in 1965 the format consisted of twenty-six lessons in two books providing two quarters of study. In this second edition this format has been continued. The main lines of the earlier work have been retained. The second edition has provided the opportunity to sharpen certain aspects of the study and to share new insights and understandings with the readers.

The first book contains two lessons of introductory material which include backgrounds, approaches to the book, study suggestions and principles of interpretation. Also included is a brief list of suggested readings. Each lesson has a list of study questions in which expressions of differences of opinion have been encouraged.

This writer does not think he has all the answers concerning this Biblical book, nor does he think any other writer has. This is one of the values of studying the book together. He does hope, however, that his comments and background materials may be of help to the student in making Revelation more understandable to many Christians. The great practical lessons to be learned from it will contribute greatly to Christian growth and maturity.

The lessons follow the chapter and verse order of Revelation with the sections of Scripture to be commented on listed at the head of each division of the lesson. The first book covers chapters one through eleven. The second book covers chapters twelve through twenty-two. If you and your class will follow the study suggestions given in Lesson Two, Revelation will be even more rewarding to you. Do not expect to find everything completely clear to your understanding in the Book of Revelation. Realize that the major lessons can be grasped even if all the details may not be clear to you. With this in mind the study of Revelation can be richly rewarding and dangerous speculations can be kept from marring the fellowship and love of the church.

A reading list of books that have proved helpful is appended at the close of Volume II on Revelation.

I am grateful for permission to quote from the books referred to in this study.

Frank Pack
Pepperdine University

TABLE OF CONTENTS

Lesson 1

INTRODUCTION (PART I)

With this lesson we begin the study of one of the most inter-esting and exciting books of the Bible. It makes its appeal to our past knowledge of the Bible, to our imaginations and to our minds, as we think together concerning the meaning of God's purpose in history. Because our understanding of its message depends so much on making the proper approach to the study, the first two lessons in this study will be devoted to discussing important background materials that will help us later when we come to the actual text of the book. Only chap-ters 1-11 are covered in this study. Due to the fact that so much material is contained in the 22 chapters, we felt that no class would wish to cover it all in so brief a period as the thir-teen lessons of a quarter would provide. Hence, the lessons have been arranged for a more detailed study of the materials of the book through two quarters.

Difficulty

The Book of Revelation, the last book in the New Testament, has probably suffered more from misuse and neglect than any other book of the Bible. Many Christians shy away from it be-cause it is certainly one of the most difficult books to under-stand. While some claim to have unraveled all its riddles, most of us feel that there are many things about it that we do not un-derstand. Because it is couched in language that is highly sym-bolic, and presents to us visions that are filled with all kinds of vivid imagery, it is mystifying to the average reader. It has become the playground of extremists and fanatics who have presented many bizarre interpretations. Many Bible scholars and commentators (such as the great reformers, Zwingli and Calvin) have refused to comment upon this book. With the exception of a few passages having special appeal, it is probably the least read of all the books of the New Testament. Some, in conversation, have actually expressed themselves as being afraid of reading it. Because some passages within it have stirred controversy and have been used as the foundations for various speculative theories, many have almost excluded it from the collection of New Testament books by their fear of studying it. Yet, no Bible student has anything to fear from the study of this book. It is the only book which contains a specific blessing to the one who reads and to those who hear the words of its prophecy and observe the things that are found therein (Rev. 1:3). Did the Holy Spirit foresee that men might neglect this book and miss the beauty and power of its message? Despite its difficulties this book offers some great blessings to those who read and grasp its message in a sane, Biblical study.

It is the conviction of the author of this study that some great values for Christians can be found in the Book of Revelation. This would seem particularly true for an age living amid tensions and turmoil throughout the world. It speaks with particular relevance to our personal needs as it emphasizes the lordship of God over his world and the affairs of man and the ultimate triumph of righteousness over the forces of evil.

What Is Its Nature?

In a way that is not characteristic of any other book of the New Testament, this book exhibits more than one type of literature. Within the opening verses of the first chapter, it is called an apocalypse (1:1), a prophecy (1:3), and an epistle (1:4-6,11). The Holy Spirit has made use of a number of different literary types in the Bible in order to convey God's message to all types of people in their needs (e.g. law, history, poetry, proverbs, etc.). We are not surprised to find this fact

2

demonstrated within the New Testament itself. However, it is unusual to find such a wonderful combination of types within one book.

Perhaps one reason we find Revelation so difficult to understand may be in the fact that it belongs to a type of literature, strange to most of us, known as apocalyptic literature but represented in the Bible by the books of Ezekiel, Daniel, and parts of Zechariah. The Greek word *apokalypsis* is translated "revelation" in the beginning of the book and literally means "an unveiling or revealing of something that has not been known before." Sometimes this book is simply called "The Apocalypse."

"Apocalyptic literature" also refers to a type of literature represented by a group of writings not found in either the Old or the New Testament. Such books as the Book of Enoch, the Ascension of Isaiah, the Assumption of Moses, and the Psalms of Solomon belong to this group of non-canonical apocalypses. There are certain common features that the non-canonical apocalypses share with those books in the Bible mentioned above, but also there are some striking differences which exist between the books of the Bible, particularly Revelation, and these non-canonical works. We shall now note these similarities and differences briefly.

All apocalyptic literature deals with the coming of the judgement and the end of all things. Its point of view is future. The predictions, however, are not in plain language but rather in visions that are highly symbolic, drawing upon nature and the life of man on earth. These convey symbolically the lesson of the vision. Angels are guides and interpreters, and through these visions some foreshadowing of the struggle of good and evil, and the triumph of God and his people are set forth.

Yet, the Biblical books that contain such imagery are very different from non-canonical books in a number of ways. While the non-canonical works do not contain the names of their real authors but are falsely entitled with forged names, the Biblical writings bear the names of the authors. Falsely claimed to be revelations from God's Spirit in a time when prophets of God no longer appeared in Israel, the non-canonical are copied imperfectly from Old Testament prophetic visions, notably from Daniel. While these emphasized that all things were in God's hands so that man could neither hasten nor delay a determined purpose of God, and were pessimistic about the present age, the Biblical writings (Ezekiel, Daniel, Revelation) do not betray this pessimism nor do they discount the importance of the human element in the fulfillment of God's purposes in history. The Book of Revelation in particular shows not only that God is in control of history, but that right and truth will triumph and that God is at work in the affairs of history to bring to realization his purposes. God will finally bring all evil under judgment, and confront all men with his absolutely righteous judgment. By means of the symbols used the great struggle of good and evil, as the church in the first century was experiencing it, is graphically set forth as a part of a total struggle going on within the universe. The outcome of this struggle has been guaranteed through Jesus Christ our Lord.

This book is not only apocalyptic in its imagery; it is also a prophecy. The author claims to be a prophet of God (22:9), one who speaks on behalf of God, and, therefore, among other powers of his prophetic office is able to predict the future and the outcome of all things (10:11; 19:10). In fact, this book is called a prophecy (1:3; 22:7, 10, 18, 19), and the same concern for faithfulness and devotion to God that makes the prophecies of the old Testament such impassioned moral and spiritual pleas likewise characterizes "the words of the prophecy of this book." As prophecy Revelation sees all men and nations subject to God's righteous purposes and calls them to repentance and obedience. It warns of the outcome of disobedience both to the church and to the world. Regardless of how strong or numerous the individuals or nations may become in their opposition to the moral and spiritual laws of this universe, the warfare against darkness, error, and evil must continue until the "kingdom of the world has become the kingdom of our Lord and of his Christ" (11:15). John Wick Bowman (*The Drama of*

4

the Book of Revelation, p. 11) has written, "It is also far closer to the prophetic message and to the writings of the Hebrew prophets in both spirit and content than any other of the apocalypses known to us. These latter appear, indeed, quite openly to ignore the prophets, whereas John quotes them verbatim in almost 150 separate passages!"

In addition to being apocalyptic and prophetic, Revelation is written in the form of an epistle. While it contains seven letters, each one addressed to one of the seven churches of Asia, there is no evidence that these letters ever existed individually or that this part of the book was separated from the rest of it. Instead, these letters form a part of the whole book and, no doubt, the entire work was sent to all of these churches. Following the blessing for its being read aloud (1:3, see Col. 4:16), it begins with the conventional salutation of a letter after the first three introductory verses, giving the author's name (1:4). It also ends characteristically as a letter (22:21). Revelation is a remarkable book combining the pictures and imagery of apocalypse, with enough prophecies to make it a truly prophetic book in the form of an epistle.

Symbolism

As is characteristic of apocalyptic literature, the Book of Revelation abounds in rich imagery drawn from all aspects of nature and human life. The horse, the lion, leopard, bear, lamb, calf, locusts, scorpion, eagle, vulture, fish, frogs, trees, harvest, and vintage all appear in the visions of the book. In addition, the description of human life, particularly the life and trade of great cities, is very full. While no direct quotations from the Old Testament in any extended way occur, there are many allusions to its imagery so that the book can be said to be saturated with the thought of the Old Testament. H. B. Swete has estimated that out of the 404 verses of the book, 278 of them contain references to Old Testament Scriptures *(The Apocalypse of St. John*, p. cxi). In addition, there are many figures that occur only in this book, such as the vision of the woman and the man child in chapter twelve. While in many

5

places the writer interprets the meaning of the symbols, in other places the reader is left to make his own interpretation.

One of the most important aspects of the symbolism of Revelation is its frequent and symbolic use of numbers. The following numbers occur: two, three, three and one-half, four, five, six, seven, ten, twelve, twenty-four, forty-two, one hundred and forty-four, six hundred and sixty-six (or, according to some manuscripts in Rev. 13:18, six hundred and sixteen), one thousand, one thousand two hundred and sixty, one thousand six hundred, seven thousand, one hundred and forty-four thousand, one hundred million, and two hundred million. The predominant number in the book is seven. It occurs fifty-four times. The next is twelve, with multiples of twelve very common (such as twenty-four, one hundred and forty-four, one thousand two hundred and sixty, one hundred and forty-four thousand). Four occurs fairly often, with three less prominent. It should be noted that four added to three make seven, while four times three make twelve. The number three is associated with the Father, the Son, and the Holy Spirit in the Godhead and elsewhere in Scripture is connected with the world, the major points of the compass, and the forces of the universe. It also symbolizes the completeness of the square with its four sides. Six is a number associated with man and his endeavors, for man was created on the sixth day (Gen. 1:27). Undoubtedly, the use of numbers in this fashion is intended to convey a special meaning. About this we shall have more to say as we study the text of the book.

Authorship and Date

The writer identified himself by name, "His (God's) servant John," and used his personal name three times in the first chapter (1:1, 4, 9). He described himself as "your brother and companion in tribulation" (1:9) and placed himself among the prophets of the New Testament period (22:9). Yet the true author of this book is Jesus Christ (1:1) who revealed the things found in this book to his servant, John. These are the things which God has given to Christ to declare to his followers. Thus the authority of the book is the highest possible as it goes through John to Jesus Christ to God the Father himself.

The testimony of the tradition from the second century A.D. is overwhelming in identifying the John mentioned here as John, the son of Zebedee, one of the twelve apostles. Justin Martyr clearly ascribed it to the apostle John about A.D. 135, and Irenaeus (about A.D. 185) quotes frequently from it as the writing of the apostle John. Mention is made of it in the Muratorian Canon (about A.D. 170) as addressed to seven churches but speaking to all the churches. Tertullian, Clement of Alexandria, Origen, and Hippolytus of Rome, in the early third century A.D. all accepted it as apostolic. However, in the middle of the third century Dionysius of Alexandria felt that there were such great differences in the style and language of this book and the Gospel of John that the two could not have been written by the same individual. Dionysius accepted the gospel as apostolic, but felt this book might possibly have been written by some other individual bearing the same name. It has been pointed out that while John identifies himself by name, he nowhere in the book calls himself an apostle. Those who have rejected the apostolic authorship have endeavored to identify John as the elder, referred to by Eusebius. This theory, however, rests only upon the possibility that the memory of John the elder completely disappeared from the church in the second century, and mistakenly the church identified John as the apostle. It is difficult to see how one whose authority and prominence was so great in Asia Minor that he could simply call himself "John" without further introduction could be forgotten so soon. It must be admitted that there are striking differences in the language and style of the Book of Revelation and the gospel of John.

Yet there are also striking similarities between this book and other Johannine writings. The use of certain titles applied to Christ, the use of certain words common to both the Gospel and the Greek of Revelation, the use of certain phrases and expressions found only in these two works, and a number of

7

words in a common vocabulary exhibited by both works, as well as the style of writing and sentence structure have been pointed out. In addition, the major theme of conflict between the powers of good and evil, the forces of light and darkness, is seen in both the Gospel and the book of Revelation.

One of the characteristics of this book is the irregularities of the Greek language. Rules of the Greek language are broken in one place and followed in other passages within the book. Some of these irregularities can be explained as reflecting an Aramaic origin or background. C. C. Torrey advocated this view, holding that the book was translated from Aramaic into Greek with great literalness, and by this he accounted for some of the unique constructions which he states resemble the type of thing one finds in Aquila's translation of the Old Testament into Greek. Many scholars do not find the language differences sufficient to outweigh the similarities that exist between the writing of the gospel and this book. Modern scholarship remains divided on the problem, with most conservative scholars acknowledging the apostle John as the author of the book in line with the overwhelming testimony of tradition reaching back to the period immediately following its writing.

Two views have been taken toward the date. The traditional date toward the end of the reign of Domitian (81-96) rests upon the statement of Irenaeus, writing about A.D. 185. "For it was seen, not a long time ago, but almost in our own generation, at the end of the reign of Domitian" (Her.v, 30:3). This is the testimony given by other early church fathers, including Eusebius. However, in recent years the Nero theory has arisen, partly to explain the differences in style between the Gospel of John and Revelation, and partly because Rev. 17:9 is thought to refer to Nero as the fifth ruler. Some have interpreted the number 666 (13:18) as spelling out the name of Nero Caesar in Hebrew numerology and have argued that this would place the writing of the book between 68 and 70, just at the end of Nero's rule. But the situation among the churches as reflected in this book as well as the general circumstances of the time are better explained in the time of Domitian than in that of

Nero, and weight of tradition is overwhelming for the later date.

Purpose and Message

The purpose of the book has been differently stated by different writers according to their approach. It seems to this writer that the primary purpose, in showing the churches the things that must come to pass hereafter, is to encourage and assure them, amid persecutions, of their ultimate victory and the victory of the cause of Christ. Though they are few in number, poor, and distressed, yet the mighty forces of evil will not overwhelm them, for Christ has conquered and guarantees their ultimate triumph. Yet, they are realistically told that they must suffer, that more persecutions await them, and that the Lord demands of them faithfulness to his will in spite of all the pressures that may come.

The book also has the purpose of showing the struggles of God's people against evil through the ages, dramatized in the symbols of opposition and persecution that are found within. It focuses attention upon the "last days" when God's justice will be evidenced and the cause of his people fully vindicated as well. One cannot escape the view that a number of times one is taken to the end-time and allowed to see under various figures the conclusion of the world order, and the promises to the faithful of their victory.

As its message tremendously encouraged the churches of Asia, which second century writings show, it has always spoken a special message to Christians in times of perplexity and conflict. Though couched in symbols which may sometimes seem strange to us, its message is a very relevant one to our time. It calls us to stand firmly and courageously with the Lamb in his great struggle with the dragon, Satan. It inspires courage strengthens faith that we might patiently endure in hope. It assures the church of its place in the purposes of God and of the victory of his people. It reminds us once more that the ultimate triumph of righteousness will not be brought about through some kind of gradual evolution toward a perfect society, but will be brought about by the return of our Lord Jesus Christ. In no other book in the New Testament is there such encouragement for Christians who face a world order where the odds seem so greatly against them. (For further discussion of its practical lessons for Christians today, see lesson 13 in the second book of Lessons on Revelation.)

Summary

We have noticed the difficulty many Christians have encountered in studying this book and the fear others have had lest, in studying it, they should be led away from the faith through bizarre interpretations. Through the blessing pronounced upon the one reading and those hearing and keeping the words of the prophecy of the book we have seen the value God places upon its study and the wisdom of its inclusion in the group of New Testament books. Three types of literature are illustrated in the book: apocalypse, prophecy, and epistle. The many references to the Old Testament, the symbols drawn from nature and human life, and the frequent use of numbers symbolically, have been pointed out. We have briefly noted the evidence for and against the apostolic authorship by John, son of Zebedee, and some of the peculiarities of the original language of Revelation. The additional backgound, questions of date, purpose and value have prepared us for the next lesson in which our attention will be focused upon how the book has been interpreted and its overall view.

Discussion Questions

1. What are some of the reasons why people have been reluctant to study the Book of Revelation? Do you think that it is profitable to make an extended study of this book even if one cannot understand fully all of the symbols?

2. What blessing to the reader and hearer of this book is stated in the text?

3. What speculations and controversies have been stirred up over interpreting the Book of Revelation?

4. Why do you think the Holy Spirit made use of different types of literature in communicating God's will to men?

5. Describe some characteristics of apocalyptic literature. What similarities and differences exist between Revelation and non-canonical (not in the canon)? (See Lightfoot's *How We Got Our Bible* for additional information on the canon.)

6. What distinctions can be drawn between ordinary prophecy and apocalyptic literature? What characteristics of an epistle do you see in Revelation?

7. Can you think of any significance for the meaning of the book in its exhibiting these three types of literary form?

8. How closely related to the Old Testament is it? As you read through this book, be on the lookout for various references to Old Testament figures and ideas.

9. How are numbers used in the book?

10. What evidence may be given for the apostolic authorship of the book? What objections are made against this position?

11. After reading the section about its purpose, state in your own words the purpose of the book.

12. What message can we look for in its teachings?

Lesson 2

INTRODUCTION (PART II)

This lesson continues the background materials for the study of the Book of Revelation begun in the previous lesson. Attention will be focused upon the major approaches in interpreting the book that have dominated its history in the past and continue to be represented in present day writings. Both strength and weaknesses of these approaches will be pointed out. This lesson also contains a statement of the major principles that should guide us in properly interpreting the Book of Revelation. Since the major disagreements have arisen over how it should be interpreted, these principles should be very carefully thought about. In addition, there is included a brief outline of the entire book along with a short suggested reading list and some study suggestions.

Major Theories of Interpretation

The approach one follows in interpreting this book is more crucial than in any other book of the New Testament because of the unity of its material. The point of view one takes at the beginning colors one's interpretation throughout Revelation. It is not surprising that through the centuries of church history there have developed widely different theories of interpreting this book. While there have been many points of view expressed in commentaries and other writings, all of them tend to group themselves into about four major categories. These are called the futurist, the preterist, the continuous historical, and the symbolic or philosophy of history views.

The futurist theory sees this book dealing with the events at the end of this world. The futurists pride themselves on being literalists in their interpretation of the book, taking its numbers as true mathematical values without symbolic meaning, and taking the other symbols in the book as literal. This view is generally associated with premillennialism which looks forward to a thousand years' reign of Christ on earth. At the present time, it is most completely expressed in the form of premillennialism known as dispensationalism. This system is set forth in the notes of the *Scofield Reference Bible*. Chapters 4-19 are interpreted as giving a blueprint for the seven years of "the rapture" (the catching up of the saints to meet Christ in the air) which they think immediately precedes the beginning of the millennium on earth (1 Thess. 4:13-18.) These seven years are the period described in Daniel 9:24-27 as the seventieth week. It is separated from the other 69 weeks by many centuries because the Jewish rejection of Jesus as the Christ automatically stopped the fulfillment of God's plan and postponed it, till this seven year period immediately before the coming of Christ to earth. The messages addressed to the seven churches in chapters two and three are thought to represent stages of church history, rather than genuine letters. Chapter 20 describes the descent of Christ to earth to begin his millennial reign. Among many things that can be said by way of objection to premillennialism, the futurist view completely separates the book from the first century church to whom it was addressed and the problems that the early church confronted. The book is entirely concerned with the end of time. Thus, it would have very little meaning and consolation to offer to those who were enduring the hardships of the first century. It is true that the book does deal in part with the events of the end and the final triumph of God and his people. The futurist theory does emphasize that the Book of Revelation points toward the end, and allows one to view that consummation a number of times within the book.

The second theory, commonly called the preterist, holds that the book is completely past. It was addressed to the contemporary first century Christians and all of its message was fulfilled in the period before Constantine. Arising out of the conditions of the Roman Empire, with persecution of the early church, its entire message is to be found in the struggles of the church with the forces of evil represented by that empire. It stands as a kind of literary and historical monument to the church of that time, but is no longer prophecy but rather past history to us. It contains little by way of message to the church of the present day. This viewpoint makes the element of prophecy mentioned in the book of little importance, but it does have the strong value of making Revelation very meaningful and encouraging to first century Christians. It runs into the difficulty, if followed without modification, that there are passages within the book that seem unmistakably to point to the future, taking one up to the end-time. To put it entirely in the past seems to fly in the face of the materials in the book itself. This author finds it hard to think that the message of the Book of Revelation regards the consummation and triumph of the book to be related to the official recognition of Christianity under the Roman Emperor Constantine. To any person who believes that there occurred a gradual falling away from the New Testament faith, it is highly unlikely that the Book of Revelation celebrates the victory of Christianity over paganism in the union of church and state under Emperor Constantine. The preterist position puts the stamp of divine approval on the church-state union which requires infant baptism for it to be effective.

A third and very popular school of interpretation among Protestants, particularly since the Reformation, has been the continuous historical theory which looks upon the book as a blueprint of the history of Western Europe from the time of John to the second coming of Christ. It conceives the visions to follow one another in chronological fashion and focuses the primary attention of the book upon the Roman Catholic church and its apostasy in the papacy. Commentators have worked out the patterns of historical happenings with great detail, paralleling these to the visions of the book. This view has been popularized by such leading Protestant commentators as Albert Barnes, Adam Clarke, B. H. Carroll, and a number of others who have written commentaries on this book, following their lead. Most of the Protestant Reformers identified Papal Rome with the beast and Babylon the Great. Alexander Campbell used one of his propositions.in the debate against Bishop Purcell based upon this position. While it has the value of focusing our attention upon the struggles within history between good and evil, its weakness lies in limiting God's interest to the events of Western Europe to the exclusion of all the rest of the world. It has the additional weakness of removing the major message of the book from the time of the first century Christians so that one wonders how it would have had any real meaning to them at all. While often ingenious in its identifications of historical events with the symbols in the book, those who hold this theory have found it necessary to reshuffle their interpretations of symbols as additional outstanding historical events have taken place. Their interpretation always places the current generation of interpreters in the last age before the second coming of Christ. This is the position to which they are mainly forced, despite the fact that the New Testament clearly says no one knows the day or the hour of his coming (Mark 13:31).

The fourth view is sometimes spoken of as the symbolic or the philosophy of history view. Holding that the book is concerned to inspire courage in the church in its constant struggle with evil throughout the ages, this theory does not apply its message to any specific historical age, but rather sees the symbols as simply a series of visionary descriptions of God's triumph over evil.

The reader can see that no one theory exhausts the meaning of this book. In all probability the key is to be found in combining elements from more than one. It is the point of view of this writer that the book is firmly rooted in its own time and spoke its message to the needs of its first readers. Thus, he shares with the preterist the need to see it against the background of the first century. He also holds that there are several places in the book where it would appear that we are brought to view the consummation of all things and to see the end-time under different aspects. While no continuous blueprint of history is here, he finds this book embodying principles that are relevant in various ages of the history of the church and sharing its struggle with evil. He sees its relevance to us as we live today, assuring us that God's will is destined to be victorious in history and at its consummation.

Principles of Interpretation

The student will be helped greatly in understanding this book if certain basic principles of interpretation are kept in mind. These are:

1. The Bible is the best and basic interpreter of itself. All guidance that the Book of Revelation gives to its own meaning should be followed. Its interpretation of symbols should be carefully attended.

2. The larger context should always interpret the immediate context since the Bible possesses unity. Out of this larger context, the immediate context of any passage can be taken carefully into consideration. To attempt to understand one isolated unit apart from the whole is to misinterpret the book.

3. The historical background, purpose, style of writing, and other background matters should be taken into consideration.

4. The New Covenant should be allowed to interpret the Old Covenant. Revelation used Old Testament terminology with New Testament meanings.

5. The prophetic nature of Revelation should be noted. As a prophet John was more concerned with spiritual principles than detailed prediction.

6. Because this is a book of visions and pictures, presented in a dramatic fashion, it should be understood to have a symbolic meaning. Full attention must be given to the pictorial and dramatic in this book.

7. One should get the total meaning of the vision, or series of visions, without pressing details.

8. Do not make the difficult passages in the book the key to the meaning of the entire book. Keep searching for the answers to the proper meaning of these passages.

9. While this book was primarily addressed to first century Christians, it contains a specific blessing to everyone who reads and to everyone who hears its message (1:3). It addresses the entire Christian age and covers it, but not in continuous succession. The principle of recapitulation holds that the book looks at the same period and the same events under different aspects in its different parts. For instance, the final judgment seems to be referred to in 6:12-17; 11:15-18; 14:14-20; 16:17-21; 20:11-15.

10. The principle of prolepsis or anticipation shows itself in this book. Prolepsis is defined by Milligan as "the tendency of the writer to anticipate in earlier sections, by mere allusion, what he is only to explain at a later point of his revelation" (*Lectures on the Apocalypse*, p.114). For instance, the second death mentioned in 2:11 is not explained until 20:14. This is another way of saying that the book itself is one of the best interpreters to its ideas.

Outline

I. Title and Salutation (1:1-8)
   A. The Title of the Book (1:1-3)
   B. The Salutation and Doxology (1:4-6)
   C. The Second Coming (1:7,8)

II. John's Vision of Christ (1:9-20)

III. The Letters to the Seven Churches (2,3)
   A. To Ephesus (2:1-7)
   B. To Smyrna (2:8-11)
   C. To Pergamum (2:12-17)

D. The Dragon Attacks the Woman (12:13-17)
E. The First Beast (13:1-10)
F. The Second Beast (13:11-18)
G. Understanding 666 (13:18)

VIII. The Seven Visions of the Son of Man (14:1-20)
A. The Lamb and the 144,000 (14:1-5)
B. The First Angel (14:6,7)
C. The Second Angel (14:8)
D. The Third Angel (14:9-11)
E. The Blessed Dead (14:12,13)
F. The Fourth Angel (14:14-16)
G. The Fifth Angel (14:17-20)

IX. The Seven Angels of God's Wrath (15:1-16:21)
A. The First Vision: The Sea of Glass (15:2-4)
B. The Second Vison: The Angels with the Bowls (Vials) (15:5-8)
C. The First Bowl (Vial) (16:1,2)
D. The Second Bowl (Vial) (16:3)
E. The Third Bowl (Vial) (16:4-7)
F. The Fourth Bowl (Vial) (16:8,9)
G. The Fifth Bowl (Vial) (16:10,11)
H. The Sixth Bowl (Vial) (16:12-16)
I. The Seventh Bowl (Vial) (16:17-21)

X. The Fall of Babylon the Great, the Beast, and the False Prophet (17:1-19:21)
A. The Vision of the Great Harlot (17:1-5)
B. The Beast Interpreted (17:6-11)
C. The Horns and Woman Interpreted (17:12-18)
D. Babylon's Fall Announced (18:1-3)
E. The Call to God's People (18:4,5)
F. The Threefold Cry Over Her Fall (18:9-20)
G. The Completeness of Her Fall (18:21-24)
H. The Hallelujah Chorus After Her Fall (19:1-10)
I. The Rider on the White Horse (19:11-21)

Suggestions

The following suggestions will make the study of this book more meaningful.

1. Encourage each student to add to the materials offered in this study by purchasing one or more of the books suggested in "Suggested Reading List" at the end of Volume II. As one becomes more interested in the study, he will find greater value in what others have written about this book.

2. The message of Revelation will be much more interesting if we make it apply to our own lives. While some of its visions may be rather strange, and some of its language poetical, the student will be helped if he constantly asks the questions, "What is the message in this that applies to our time?"

3. In view of the above suggestion, approach the study of this book in a prayerful, reverent way, realizing that God has spoken to his people through the message of this book down through the ages, and he has an important message to give to us today.

4. Note the unity of this book and how intricately it is put together. See if you can follow out its major themes as they reappear in various sections of the book.

5. Your study of the book will be helped if each student will keep a notebook in which various questions and comments, as well as points for further study, are recorded. This preserves one's thinking on a very important part of the Scriptures and enables him to center his attention on the Scripture text itself. It also will encourage the student to contribute his own reflections in the discussions of the class.

6. The questions that accompany each lesson are primarily designed to stimulate thought and to make the student look more carefully at the text of Revelation.

7. The most important point in any Bible study is to lay aside all of one's preconceptions as to what the passage might mean in order to listen to its teaching. If one approaches this book with certain prejudices, his view will be distorted from the start. Endeavor to let the book speak its message to you.

Discussion Questions

1. Do you agree that the approach one takes to the Book of Revelation is an important matter for consideration? Why?

2. Name the four major theories of interpretation of the Book of Revelation. Can you see why each theory is given the name that it has?

3. Describe the major points of the futurist position.

4. What does the "rapture" refer to?

5. What objections can you think of to the futurist position?

6. What are the major emphases in the preterist theories?

7. What weaknesses do you see in the continuous historical theories? What strengths do you see in these?

8. Discuss the principles of interpretation suggested here. Can you think of others that should be included?

9. What is meant by the principle of recapitulation?

10. How has prolepsis been defined as it applies to Revelation?

11. What are the major divisions of this book as they have been outlined here?

12. Think of additional suggestions for study in your group. Discuss how these may help to make your class more interesting.

Lesson 3

CHRIST IN THE MIDST
OF HIS CHURCHES

(Revelation 1:1-20)

Introduction

As we pointed out in the first lesson, the Book of Revelation is a combination of a prophecy, a letter, and a series of apocalyptic visions. In no place in the book is this more clearly shown than in this first chapter. After telling what the title of the book is, and identifying it as an apocalypse and a book of prophecy in vss. 1-3, John also introduces (vss. 4-7) the salutation of the book in the ordinary form in which we find salutations in the letters in the New Testament. Following this we come to the opening vision of the book, a vision in which we see Christ walking in glory in the midst of his churches and sending his messages to the seven churches of Asia.

The Title (1:1-3)

Vs. 1. The opening line of this book gives the true title, "the Revelation of Jesus Christ." The word "revelation" (Gr. *apokalypsis)* occurs only here in this book. It was not necessarily a religious word, but referred to the revealing of any fact. However, elsewhere in the new Testament it is used to refer to the revealing of God's will to us through His word and through Jesus Christ. The line through which this revelation is given is from God to Jesus Christ to his angel to his servant John for his servants. It will be noted later in the book, however, that the angel does not figure greatly in this revelation that comes from Christ. The word translated "servant" is the common word for "slave" and denotes the ownership by Christ and the supremacy of Christ's will." "What must soon take place" tells us what the revelation concerns. Some commentators think this simply refers to the certainty of the events. This does not necessarily mean that everything in the book must soon come to pass. However, this expression presents strong evidence against the futurist position, which locates the book in the remote future.

Vs. 2. The words "testimony" and "bear witness" are common words found in John's writings. This revelation is, likewise, John's testimony to that which Jesus Christ through his angel has made known to him. "The word of God" and "the testimony of Jesus Christ" are synonymous. This expression in variant forms is found elsewhere in the book (1:9; 6:9; 12:17; 20:4).

Vs. 3. The first of the seven beatitudes in this book occurs here (1:3; 14:13; 16:15; 19:9; 20:6; 22:7, 14). This is a special blessing upon the one who reads aloud to the listening congregation the words of this prophetic book. The blessing rests upon those who "hear" and "keep" its message. What great value there is in the public reading of the word of God! So important was the public reading of the Scriptures that in later church history the reader became an official of the church. The blessedness of hearing and obeying God's word is a beatitude that is proved again and again in the lives of Christians.

Salutation (1:4-6)

The salutation here is common to epistles in the New Testament, as a look at one of Paul's letters will show (except 1st and 2nd Timothy where grace, mercy and peace are used). Here the salutation proper is combined with the traditional Christian blessing of grace and peace, with a doxology of praise. The seven churches in Asia refer to churches located in the Roman province of Asia. In the New Testament Asia never refers to the continent of Asia but to that province in the Roman Empire that included the western part of Asia Minor. That these seven churches were not the only churches in Asia can be seen by further references in the New Testament. Churches existed at Colossae (Col. 1:2), Hierapolis (Col. 4:13), Troas (Acts 20:5), Magnesia and Tralles as Ignatius' letters (about A.D. 115) show. The seven cities were located in a semi-circle with Ephesus in the center. The special place of the number "seven" as a symbol of perfection leads us to understand that these seven churches stand for the entire church, and the message of the book is addressed through them to all God's people.

In a unique way, this salutation comes from the three persons of the Godhead, from God who is here described as "him who is and who was and who is to come," the Holy Spirit described here as "the seven spirits who are before his throne." Jesus Christ is here given three titles: "the faithful witness" (one who can bear full testimony because of first-hand knowledge), "the firstborn of the dead" who guarantees our resurrection, and "the ruler of kings on earth." Through his witnessing leading to the cross and his resurrection from the dead he is ruler of the kings of earth, a position the devil promised him in the temptation but could never have fulfilled (Matt. 4:9; Luke 4:6, 7).

The beautiful doxology that closes this salutation is the first of many which are offered to Christ in this book. While the KJV reads "washed us from our sins," the RSV based upon better manuscript evidence reads "freed us from our sins." He continues to love us and freed us once for all from our sins "with his life's blood" (NEB).[1] Another blessing that flows through Jesus Christ is that we have been made a kingdom of priests to give God honor and glory (See Ex.19:6). How impor-

---

[1]KJV refers to the King James Version, ASV to the American Standard Version, RSV to the Revised Standard Version, NEB to the New English Bible, NIV to the New International Version.

tant it is for Christians to realize that every Christian is a priest to God in the New Covenant. There is no special priesthood set apart from the total group of followers of Christ. While there are different works in the body, the royal priesthood of all believers is the priesthood taught in the New Testament (1 Pet. 2:9). Only later centuries changed this Biblical teaching.

Two Announcements (1:7, 8)

Vs. 5 tells the characteristics of Christ and what Christ has done and continues to do, vs. 6 describes what Christ has made of his followers, vs. 7 will describe what Christ has yet to do. This verse announces, "he is coming with the clouds," and all will see him. To believers it is joy unspeakable, but those who have pierced him through the ages in disregard and open rebellion will "lament in remorse" (NEB) cf. Zechariah 12:10.

Vs. 8 presents the announcement of the Lord God himself. Alpha is the first letter of the Greek alphabet and Omega the last. The expression "who is and who was and who is to come" is the same terminology used in vs. 4 concerning God. The word translated "Almighty" (Gr. *pantokrator*) emphasizes God's sovereign lordship over all things. The NEB translates this word "the sovereign Lord of all." This word occurs in this book a total of nine times (1:8; 4:8; 11:17; 15:3; 16:7, 14; 19:6, 15; 21:22). Some commentators, however, hold this verse to be the personal signature of Christ himself and to refer to him. To see the eternal God holding sway as sovereign Lord over his universe and working out his eternal purpose becomes the background for all the rest of the message of this book.

John's Vision of Christ (1:9-20)

Vs. 9 The writer, John, identified himself once more and reminded his readers that he was suffering along with them as a brother and partaker in the tribulation that Roman persecution had brought. The language would indicate that he was

26

banished to the Isle of Patmos, enduring hardship in its marble quarries. Sir William Ramsay describes the banishment combined with hard labor in these words: "It was in its worst forms a terrible fate: like the death penalty it was preceded by scourging, and it was marked by perpetual fetters, scanty clothing, insufficient food, sleep on the bare ground in a dark prison, and work under the lash of military overseers" *(The Letters to the Seven Churches,* p. 85). He is here because of his preaching the word of God.

Vs. 10. This is the only mention in the New Testament of the Lord's day (Gr. *te kuriake hemera*) referring to the first day of the week as the day of the Lord's resurrection. A different expression, the day of the Lord (Gr. *hemera tou kuriou*), refers to the day of God's judgment, often to the last day. These are not to be confused. In the second century the term "Lord's Day" became the common term for the day of Christian worship, the first day of the week. Cut off from worship, John was under the Holy Spirit's influence when he heard this trumpet-like voice.

Vs. 11. John was here commanded to write what he saw and send it in a book to the seven churches. Not for his personal benefit did these visions come, but for the benefit of the churches. These were real churches with real problems in John's own day. It is grotesque interpretation to think of these churches as signifying periods of church history, as some futurists do.

Vss. 12-16. In these verses we have the description of what John saw when he turned to see who was speaking to him. The first thing he saw was seven golden lampstands. The description of the golden candlestick with its seven lamps in the tabernacle comes to mind as well as the individual lampstands found in Solomon's temple. How remarkable that the first thing he saw was these lampstands that represented the churches! In the midst of these lampstands Christ was seen. Appropriately throughout this age, until he comes in the clouds, Christ will be seen amid his churches. He knows his churches and walks in their midst. This "one like unto a son of man" calls to mind Daniel's visions (Dan. 7:13ff; 10:5ff). This term, which was our Lord's favorite term to describe himself during his earthly ministry, has a Messianic meaning from the Daniel passages and is significantly used here.

The description turns from his clothing to his person. His head and hair, "white as white wool, white as snow," symbolize his eternity and purity. Cf. Daniel 7:9. His flaming eyes penetrate and search. His glowing feet, like freshly heated brass in a furnace, show not only his strength but also his consuming judgment. His strong, commanding voice is like the roar of mighty waters. In the right hand of his ruling power are the stars, the significance of which we shall notice below. Out of his mouth came "a sharp, two-edged sword" showing the power and force of his message. A short Roman sword that was the deadly weapon of the Roman soldier was tongue-shaped and double-edged. It was a deadly weapon for close fighting, and was used by the writer of Hebrews as a symbol for the power of God's word (Heb. 4:12). His face shone like the sun shining in full blazing glory. The close parallel between the appearance of Christ on the mount of transfiguration and this vision of the glorious Christ walking amidst his churches in all his power and splendor cannot escape the reader. It must also have been in the mind of John, who experienced both of these great demonstrations of Christ's glory. (See Mark 9:2 and parallels.)

Vss. 17, 18. Several times in the Scriptures men have prostrated themselves before a demonstration of divine power and glory. (See Gen. 17:3; Ezek. 1:28; 3:23; 43:3; Dan. 8:17; 10:9; Matt. 17:6; Luke 5:8; Acts 9:4; 26:14.) "Fear not." How often does this statement occur in the consolation God gives to his people! The purpose of Christ's appearance was not to strike terror but to bring comfort and strength. Swete says, "The hand which sustains nature and the churches at the same time quickens and raises individual lives" (*The Apocalypse of St. John*, p. 19). No problem should arise in conceiving of Christ laying his right hand upon John, even though this right hand carried the seven stars, for this whole vision is symbolic and the right hand was constantly used as the hand to commission. As the first and the last, the one who died and who lives forevermore, having the keys of Death and Hades, the realm of the dead, Christ identifies himself and expresses the authority with which he commands the things that are found for his churches. Notice the "I am" statements made in this passage.

Vss. 19, 20. He repeats the command to write made in vs. 11, giving the content of the writing: what John was seeing, a glorified Christ, the things which are, the revealing of the present state of the church and Christ's message to them, and the things that must take place hereafter, referring to the future, to the consummation of God's purpose. This tells us once more the content of the book. "The mystery" refers to that which has been hidden from human reason, but disclosed and revealed by God that men might know his will. The lampstands and the stars are both interpreted. The problem here is to understand the meaning of "angel" (Gr. *aggelos,* messenger). Elsewhere this word refers to spiritual beings; some interpreters have taken it literally. But the difficulty is that the letters were addressed to the angel of each church and the angels are rebuked for and warned about the sins as well as praised for the good in the churches. Why would an angel receive a message from the Lord through an earthly messenger? Others have viewed the angel as simply an earthly messenger through whom the churches sent messages to John on the Isle of Patmos. The question that arises here is whether John can be thought of as writing a letter to those who were standing in his presence and rebuking them, as messengers, for the sins of the churches. The letters addressed to the angels seem to view a body of people that are praised and warned and called to repentance. Some interpreters think that the angels are "the pastors," or "monarchial bishops" of each church, but the above objections to previous points of view would apply as well here. In addition, the New Testament knows no use of "pastor" or "bishop" in the modern sense of one man over a church or over a group of churches. New Testament churches had a plurality of elders, who are also called bishops or pastors, these words referring to different ways in which their work may be considered. (See Acts 20:17,28; Eph. 4:11; Phil. 1:1; Titus 1:5,7.) The best view, it seems to this writer, is to take the angel as the symbol of the spiritual life of the church, as the lampstand symbolizes its outward embodiment or its visible existence. Often in the Book of Revelation there are angels of winds, fire and the abyss that symbolize objects or forces in the universe so that this interpretation is not far afield in light of the total context of this passage. One of the important principles of interpretation in understanding this book, as in every other book of the Bible, is to look carefully at the context of any passage. Seeing the way in which the angel of each church is conceived in this series of letters will help us understand better the use of the term here. Bishop Lightfoot thinks that the contrast between the heavenly fire (star) and the earthly fire (lampstand) is significant. "The star is the suprasensual counterpart, the heavenly representative; the lamp, the earthly realization, the outward embodiment." (*Epistle to the Philippians*, p. 199.)

In this lesson we have studied the verses of the first chapter. The nature of the book, what its message will relate to, and the particular blessing upon reader and hearers make up the first division. The unique form of its salutation has presented God, Christ, and the Holy Spirit in their relationship to the churches. This has been followed by a twofold announcement concerning the second coming of Christ when the consummation of God's purpose will be realized and the statement of God's sovereign lordship over all will bring these purposes to realization. Then follows the initial vision of the glorious Christ who commissions John to send the letters to the seven churches. Various descriptive phrases by which Christ is set forth in this vision will recur in connection with the letters to the churches.

Discussion Questions

1. How do the first three verses of the book show the kind of book Revelation is?

2. What is the meaning of the word "revelation"? Show how it is used elsewhere in the New Testament.

3. What is meant by "beatitude"? How would you describe the seven beatitudes of this book?

4. What evidence do we have that other churches existed besides these seven in the province of Asia at this time?

5. Discuss the three terms used in the salutation to describe Christ.

6. How are we to understand the meaning of "priests" in this passage and in the rest of the New Testament?

7. What significance for the modern world do you see in the lesson of v. 8?

8. How can the term "Son of Man" be called a Messianic term in the light of the visions of Daniel?

9. What do the various aspects of the description of Jesus in this initial vision symbolize about him?

10. What is meant by "mystery" as used here and elsewhere in the New Testament?

11. What views have been taken concerning the meaning of "angel" as used in this part of the book?

Lesson 4

THE SEVEN CHURCHES (Part I)
(Revelation 2:1-11)

Introduction

Chapters two and three give the text of the seven short letters addressed to seven churches in the Roman province of Asia. These are the churches named in 1:11 but were not the only churches in the province. There were churches at Troas (Acts 20:5), Colossae (Col. 1:2), Hierapolis (Col. 4:13), and the writings of Ignatius some 20 years later include Magnesia and Tralles. Why were these seven churches selected? Scholars have advanced various reasons for the selection. Some emphasize the fact that these churches are located on the great road that goes in a circle through the interior of the province from Ephesus and thus the churches were strategically located. Some have suggested that these were the only churches where John had done missionary work and, therefore, Christ chose to write to them through John. Others have said that only these seven bore the title of "metropolis" and were the chief cities of the postal districts of the province. Another reason advanced is that the number seven, which is so prominent in the book (occurring 54 times) and regarded as the symbol of perfection, indicates not only that these particular congregations are addressed, but the church as a whole and throughout the ages is addressed. The conditions and circumstances of the church at large are dealt with. In the Muratorian Canon, the earliest separate list of books of the new Testament with brief notes attached (about A.D. 170), the following is said: "For John also, though he wrote in the Revelation to seven churches, nevertheless speaks to them all." This latter reason seems to be the best one, particularly in light of the materials in these letters. It is evident that the letters did not circulate separately but are a part of a very important whole. In fact, the message of the whole book is addressed to these churches and, through them, to the whole church. Beckwith says, "Every great revelation, whether Old Testament prophecy or New Testament epistle, is given in view of definite contemporary and local circumstances, but it brings, in this form, truth of universal significance." (*The Apocalypse of John*, p. 447.)

Common Features

Certain common features are evident as one looks at each one of these letters. They are all dictated by the Lord himself, and each one is addressed to the angel of the specific church. Except for Laodicea, the titles by which the Lord describes himself are all drawn from the vision in ch. 1. The titles by which Christ describes himself to the Laodicean church are drawn instead from the salutation of the book (1:5, 6). A structure is common to all these epistles. While not all of the epistles possess each element, due to certain local conditions, nevertheless each letter follows this common structure; (1) salutation, (2) Christ's description of himself, (3) his appeal and warning, (6) his exhortation, "He who has an ear, let him hear what the Spirit says to the churches," (7) promise. In the last four letters the sixth and seventh elements are reversed in order. In the letters to Smyrna and Philadelphia there are no words of condemnation, while in the letter to Laodicea there are no words of commendation. A very interesting study concerning Christ and his relationship to his churches can be made in taking each one of the self-designations in the beginning of each letter and studying them consecutively. In addition, the student will find it very helpful to make a comparative chart for each church in which each one of these major points found in the letter may be put down and compared with the other epistles.

Letter to Ephesus (2:1-7)

Ephesus was the most important city in the Roman province

of Asia, which occupied the western part of what is not Asiatic Turkey. At this time, Asia was probably the most cultured province of the Roman Empire. It was the site of ancient Ionia, the seat of Greek culture and Grecian art, and its noble cities, beautiful temples and public buildings gave testimony to the Greek way of life that stretched back for centuries. Ephesus was located at the mouth of the Cayster River and was an important commercial center. Its harbor was never too good, however, and the present ruins of Ephesus are located some seven miles across marshy lowland from the Aegean Sea. Here, about the 12th century B.C., a mixed settlement of Ionian settlers and Asiatic settlers formed the first city. Later in 557 B.C. the Persians captured it and made it a part of their empire. Alexander the Great added it to his great Greek Empire, and it was later a part of the Kingdom of Pergamum, which Attalus the Third willed to Rome in 133 B.C. While Pergamum remained the capital of the province of Asia, Ephesus was the seaport and commercial center, as well as the center of the worship of Diana (Artemis). Ephesus had been sacred to the worshipers of Diana for many centuries. The temple which was dedicated to her was rebuilt after a fire in 365 B.C. and continued until 262 A.D. It was one of the seven wonders of the ancient world. Two hundred feet wide and 425 feet long, it was four times the size of the Parthenon in Athens. It had 120 columns, each one 60 feet high, and each one the gift of a king. The image of Diana in this temple was believed to have fallen from heaven (Acts 19:35), and was regarded as one of the most sacred in the ancient pagan world. The title "temple keeper of great Artemis" was one of the proud titles that this city bore. The Book of Acts points out that one of the principal businesses in this sacred place was the making of shrines sacred to Artemis (Acts 19:24). The temple was not only a place of worship, but also a place where great wealth was kept. It was a kind of ancient bank. It was also a sanctuary for criminals who found refuge here, since no one might be arrested for any crime who was within a bow shot of its walls. The type of worship that was practiced was a mixture of Greek and Oriental cultic practices, in which sacred prostitution figured. In addition, Ephesus was the center of worship to the emperors, and the officials (Asiarchs) of the imperial temples are mentioned in Acts 19:31.

Ephesus is already known to us as a principal center for early Christianity. Paul established the church here, briefly spending time during the second journey (Acts 18:19-21). On the third journey he stayed longer than he did in any other city, possibly three full years (Acts 20:31). The church grew and was so successful that its effect on paganism and the practice of magic aroused serious hostility and caused the riot described in Acts 19. While Paul was working here Christianity spread through the province. (See Acts 19:10; Col. 1:6.) To its elders he addressed a fitting farewell, warning them concerning the problems that they faced (Acts 20:17-35). To this church he addressed a letter which is commonly classed as one of the prison letters, and later sent Timothy here to carry out special responsibilities (1 Tim. 1:3). About the time of the Jewish war and the fall of Jerusalem, tradition claims that the Apostle John came from Judea to Ephesus and spent the last years of his life in that area.

In the salutation Christ describes himself as holding the seven stars in his right hand walking in the midst of his churches. He holds their spiritual life in his grasp and he is close to all of his churches. In this first letter he reminds them that he knows his churches, and his knowledge is borne out in the letters that follow. He praises their "toil" and their "patient endurance," an endurance that bore up under all kinds of difficulties, suffering, and struggle, without growing weary (vs. 3). In another way this church received the praise of the Lord, because they tested those calling themselves "apostles," a term used of wandering missionaries, and had found them to be false. Paul had warned them against false teachers (Acts 20:29) and the New Testament points out the need for testing the faithfulness of those who would teach (1 John 4:1-3). Ephesus had taken Paul's warning to heart, and had not only watched against false teachers but hated "the works of the Nicolaitans, which I also hate" (vs. 6). Just who the Nicolaitans were we do not know, since they are not identified here.

They are mentioned again in vs. 15 in the letter to Pergamum, and are closely identified with those who hold the teaching of Balaam. Apparently they were those who were teaching that it was all right to compromise with the world, to engage in the heathen festivals as Christians, since this would have nothing to do with damaging the soul. They partook possibly of that form of popular error that made a radical distinction between flesh and spirit, and felt that nothing done by the flesh could have any effect on the spirit. In this way they could justify their compromising immoralities. Irenaeus, Hippolytus, and Clement of Alexandria (second century A.D.) all mentioned them as following lives of self-indulgence. The Ephesian church had vigorously opposed their false teaching.

Yet the Lord had something against this church, for toil, patient endurance, and soundness of doctrine are not all that he requires of his people. They had "abandoned the love you had at first." It can hardly mean that they had left the faith for some doctrinal error as some have thought. This may mean that they had cooled in their enthusiasm and ardor for Christianity, but this does not seem likely in view of their toil and their patient endurance. It probably refers to the fact that their love for one another, their spirit of genuine devotion and Christian brotherhood had cooled. They had allowed the spirit of censoriousness and fault-finding with one another to stifle the true spirit of love. In looking for heresy it is easy to fall into the pitfall of spiritual poverty and barren conformity. What an excellent lesson for the church today! When love of brethren cools, love for God cannot long flourish. They are intimately related. (Read 1 John 4:7-21). The appeal of Christ involves three things: remember, repent, and do. Remembering what they once were and the position from which they have fallen as a church can lead them then to repent. Repentance involves the recognition that we have sinned and the change of will which makes us resolve to do God's will instead of our own (2 Cor. 7:10). The evidence of it, the fruits of it, will show in their doing "the works you did at first." Theirs is the job of learning again to do what they once did and then forgot. How often is that the case with us! The Lord's threat to them is that he will come quickly and their lampstand will be removed unless they repent. The coming of the Lord probably does not refer primarily to the second coming at the judgment of the last day, but to a preliminary visitation of God's judgment upon an impenitent people. Vs. 7 introduces the first instance of the formula that is common to all the seven messages. It sounds very much like one of the familiar sayings of Christ found in the Gospels. (See Matt. 11:15; 13:9, 43; Mark 4:9, 23; Luke 8:8; 14:35.) It might be pointed out that though Christ is speaking, it is the Spirit that is identified with him who is saying this message to the churches through the prophet John. The same close relation of Christ and the Holy Spirit is seen in 2 Corinthians 3:17. This exhortation reminds us that while each church receives a specific message, the other churches are to heed the message as it may apply to them. Though the letter is addressed to the church, and it is spoken of as a whole, the promise that is given is addressed specifically to each individual Christian. The one who conquers, who is faithful to the end, is a victorious one. To eat of the tree of life means to partake of life everlasting, which man forfeited in his sin in Eden. Christ restores what Adam lost for man. Yet it depends on individual faithfulness to share in this blessedness. Concerning paradise, which is a word brought from Persian into Greek, meaning literally a park or garden, Swete points out: "In the New Testament paradise is either the state of the blessed dead (Luke 23:43) or a supra-mundane sphere, identified with the third heaven into which men pass in an ecstasy (2 Cor. 12:2ff) or, as here, the final joy of the saints in the presence of God in Christ." (*The Apocalypse of St. John,* p. 30.)

Letter to Smyrna (2:8-11)

Smyrna was located to the north of Ephesus about 35 miles, with an excellent harbor at the head of a deep gulf of the Aegean Sea. Because of the beauty and safety of its harbor, it was called the Port of Asia. It had been founded as a Greek city by Lysimachus in the third century B.C., and had grown to be what Lucian called "the fairest city of Ionia." It was the natural outlet for the trade route from the interior that led

37

through the Hermus Valley. Its climate was lovely, and it was a delightful place to live. It was laid out in rectangles with well-paved streets, and its most famous street was the Street of Gold that ran from the Temple of Zeus to the Temple of Cybele. The hill that rose behind the city was crowned with beautiful temples and public buildings, and it was called "the crown of Smyrna." It had long been noted for its devotion of Rome, and had erected a temple to the goddess Roma, the personification of Rome, in 195 B.C. Cicero called Smyrna "one of our most faithful and our most ancient allies." It is not strange that it should become a center for the worship of the emperor in the New Testament period. It also attracted a large Jewish population whose hostility to the early Christians is evidenced in this letter.

In the salutation Christ describes himself as the one who was dead and lived again (1:18), no doubt to encourage them in their times of testing and suffering. Their Lord had overcome death as the living Lord. This was a church that had undergone real persecution and from the letter it would appear that their real enemies were the local Jews who prided themselves on their blood and heritage but were not real Jews (Rom. 2:28ff). They are instead "a synagogue of Satan" in their blasphemy, speaking against Christ and his followers. Our Lord knows this church in its persecution. It has gone through affliction, it has endured poverty and imprisonment. Though they were poor, yet they were rich in spiritual things. Probably they were poor due to the pillaging of their property by either hostile Jews or pagans.

The Lord does not promise his followers, though faithful and devoted, that they will escape sufferings and even physical death. As their leader he did not escape suffering and death on the cross for their salvation. "A disciple is not above his teacher" (Matt. 10:24). Instead he calls upon them not to be afraid, but to be faithful regardless of what they may face. Verse 10 reminds them that the devil is the real source of their persecution, a point that will be made abundantly clear later on in the book. This is one of those proleptic elements which were mentioned as a prominent feature of the book in the rules of interpretation. The devil makes use of the civil authorities and the ready hearts of those who blaspheme and persecute in order to imprison and cause suffering to the Christians. "Ten days" is simply a symbol for the time of their persecution, limited though severe, but short in comparison to eternity. "Be faithful" (literally, "go on being faithful") to the extent (Gr. *achri*) of the extreme penalty of death. The promise of the Lord is that he will give them everlasting life as a crown.

The word "crown" is the word used in Greek for the wreath of victory which the runners in the races received when they won. The promise to the one who overcomes is that he will not be "hurt by the second death." In order to understand the meaning of the term "the second death," one must look to the final chapters of the book (20:6, 14: 21:8). In the latter references, the second death is the same as being cast into the lake that burns with fire and brimstone, which is another way of saying that one who shrinks from the sufferings of persecution and physical death for the sake of Christ will be separated eternally from God's fellowship and will be under God's condemnation. Elsewhere in the New Testament, the eternal destiny of the wicked is decribed as death (Rom. 6:23). Obviously this is not a reference to physical death but spiritual death. The unbeliever who comes to physical death will also experience a "second death," as eternal separation from the fellowship and blessings of God (cf. 2 Thess. 1:9). The student can multiply the passages in the New Testament describing the destiny of the unbelieving and disobedient. This is not a popular teaching today, for many hold that the punishment of the wicked will only be remedial and all will ultimately be saved. Universalism has become popular among many religious people. Others hold to the idea of annihilation, but the teaching of the New Testament points out the reality of eternal separation from God and lays upon Christians the need for proclaiming to men the gospel of Christ which can redeem them in this world for life everlasting. Smyrna, the persecuted church, is not condemned for any fault, worldly, unloving persons, or else has kept the church from being filled with such persons.

Discussion Questions

1. What theories have been advanced concerning the selection of these seven churches to receive the letters? What seems the best reason to you?

2. Upon what grounds are we justified in thinking of these letters as also addressed to all the churches rather than to each one separately?

3. Study carefully the titles by which Christ addresses the churches at Ephesus and Smyrna, and note the relationship of these to the vision in ch. 1.

4. What elements of common structure do these letters possess?

5. Describe the historical background of Ephesus. What religious practices are connected with Ephesus?

6. What do we know about the earlier history of this church? Make use of the New Testament references to help with your answer.

7. How is the term "apostle" used in vs. 2? Can you locate other New Testament passages where it is used and applied to persons other than the 12 apostles? How are we then to understand the meaning of this term?

8. What guidance does the New Testament give in testing the faithfulness of teachers, preachers, and elders?

9. Who were the Nicolaitans and what positions did they probably hold?

10. To what do you think the expression "their first love" refers? Discuss this point.

11. To what does the coming of the Lord refer in vs. 5?

12. Give the historical background of Smyrna. How is this knowledge helpful in understanding the contents of this brief letter?

13. What is meant by the expression "the synagogue of Satan"?

14. Discuss the meaning of "the second death." What is meant by universalism and annihilation?

15. How do you relate the experience of these churches to the churches today?

Lesson 5

THE SEVEN CHURCHES (Part II)
(Revelation 2:12-29)

Letter to Pergamum (2:12-17)

Pergamum was the administrative capital of the Roman province of Asia and had enjoyed the distinction of being a capital city for hundreds of years. It was the center of the kingdom of Pergamum which was bequeathed to the Roman government in 133 B.C. It was here that the writing material we commonly call parchment was developed and the name of this material is derived from the name of the city. It was situated 55 miles northeast of Smyrna on a rocky hill in the Caicus Valley. Pliny spoke of it as "by far the most famous city in Asia." About 240 B.C. the Pergamenes won a great victory over the savage, invading Gauls, and to commemorate this victory built a great altar to Zeus (Jupiter) in front of the temple consecrated to Athena. Built on a ledge of rock, it looked like a great throne and from its altar the smoke of sacrifices rose every day. This may be part of what is meant by the expression "where Satan's throne is." It was also sacred to the god Dionysus, the god of wine, whose cult was quite widespread in the ancient world. It was sacred to Asclepius, the god of healing, whose symbol was the wand and coiled serpents, still used as a symbol of the medical profession. R. H. Charles has called Pergamum the Lourdes of the ancient world, due to the healing that went on here. In addition, it was the first city in Asia to establish emperor worship, and the temple dedicated "to the divine Augustus and the goddess

Roma" became the center of the worship of the emperor. During the reign of Domitian (A.D. 81-96) emperor worship became a test of loyalty to the Empire. In all probability this latter fact, even more than the other pagan religions, accounts for its description as "where Satan's throne is." The name of the city occurs in two forms, Pergamos and Pergamum, the latter being most often found in writings and inscriptions. This is the northernmost of the seven cities, with the remaining cities being located in a southeast direction from Pergamum. Laodicea, the last of these cities, is located on the great main road that went through the center of Asia Minor and terminated at Ephesus.

By virtue of the location of this church, it had some particular problems. Bowman (*Drama of the Book of Revelation*, p. 31) thinks that this church and the two that follow form a trio representing courtship, seduction, and death respectively, under Satan's influence. It is at Pergamum that we see this activity going on in the church.

After describing himself as the one who has the sharp, two-edged sword (coming from his mouth), Christ commends this church for holding fast to his name and not denying the faith, despite the place where it lives. The term "throne" occurs 45 times in this book. In the New Testament it is used to signify the seat or chair of state for kings, for God, Christ, the 12 apostles as judges, and in this instance indicates that Satan holds his court here and is enthroned here. The fact that both Zeus and Asclepius bore the title of savior in contrast to Jesus would indicate how strong paganism was here. It was also the center of emperor worship representing as a god a ruler whose evil persecuting policy against the church was so devastating. The Lord knows and understands how difficult it is for the church to live in this kind of an environment. The test was particularly severe when "Antipas my witness, my faithful one" was killed. The word here translated "witness" (Gr. *martus*) almost has come by this time to have the technical meaning of one who crowns his testimony by giving his life for his faith. Jesus is called the faithful witness (1:5), and Antipas who gave his life for Christianity is called by the same glorious title. How Antipas died we do not know. The legends that have arisen about this probably have come from later imaginings. It was certainly not an easy thing to be a Christian in Pergamum, with the strong pagan influences at the very seat of Satan's power. Pressures must have been great to compromise and to tolerate such compromise.

In condemning this church, however, he found those who were Nicolaitans probably led by a "prophet" whom he calls Balaam, because it was Balaam, the Old Testament prophet, who encouraged Balak, King of Moab, to entice Israel after his own attempts to curse Israel failed. He taught Balak how to cause Israel to engage in fornication and idolatry through the seductive women (Num. 25:1-5; 31:16), the same two sins that specifically are associated with the teaching of the Nicolaitans. In encouraging people to eat at the table of the gods, they were compromising with the idolatry of the time, which the New Testament condemns (1 Cor. 10:20ff). This is the same teaching fostered by Jezebel and her disciples at Thyatira. One of the biggest temptations is to compromise with the world by watering Christianity down instead of lifting the world up to the Christian standards. The difficulty that early Christians confronted was particularly acute here. Many worked where pagan gods were worshipped and to fail to eat and drink in their honor would bring judgment upon the group as a whole. The pressure to feast on the meal offered to idols and sacrifice to the gods became tremendous at times. The Lord's call to repent carries with it the threat that he will come in a special visitation of judgment against them and make war against them with the sharp sword of his word. Often in this book Christ is spoken of as a warrior. He makes war against those who are his enemies; in this case, those who are the false teachers. The entire church is called to repentance because of its spirit of compromise.

He promises the "hidden manna," the food at God's own heavenly banquet table, in contrast to the pagan banquets, and he also promises the white stone inscribed with the new

44

name that no one knows except the one who receives it. Several interpretations of the white stone have been advanced: (1) a small stone used for counting or voting, in which the white stone signified acquittal while the black one signified guilt; (2) a white stone refers to a little stone tablet upon which something was written. Sometimes these were given to the victorious athlete at a game and sometimes to an outstanding gladiator; (3) others have referred it to the tickets that were given for food and drink to victors in the games, entitling them to eat at public expense; (4) some have related it to the stones on the Jewish high priest's breastplate, with the names of the tribes of Israel on them; (5) others have seen no particular significance in this except that it was simply the stone on which the new name for the victor was inscribed; (6) others see white as symbolic of victory itself. At any rate, it probably refers to the high honor which the Lord will give to him as one of his own and a new nature (name) that is known only to the one who is victorious, and made pure in heaven.

Letter to Thyatira (2:18-29)

This is the longest of the seven letters. Thyatira was not a very important city, although in the earlier time it had acted as a kind of frontier city. After 189 B.C. it declined until the time of Claudius, when it began to be revived as a center of trade and manufacture. It seems to have been the center of a number of trade guilds, which were associations of people employed in certain trades, in particular, dyeing, cloth-making, pottery, and brass-making, much as we find trade unions and trade associations today. In fact, more guilds were known (through the inscriptions that have been discovered) to exist here than in any other city of Asia. Lydia was a seller of purple from Thyatira (Acts 16:14). These guilds had common meals, often held in some temple or in a place where some sacrifice was offered to a patron god or goddess. Drunken revelry often accompanied their feasts. The city seems to have had no specific religious significance.

In addressing this church Christ calls himself "the Son of

God," a title found nowhere else in this book, although implied. His eyes are "like a flame of fire," his feet "like burnished bronze," (cf. 1:14, 15) as he sees and treads upon those who oppose him in powerful judgment. Many things about this church the Lord commended: its love, faith, ministry, patient endurance, and the fact that its last works were larger than its first works. It is interesting to note that the "works" here are the love, faith, ministry, and patient endurance of this church. Here was a church that was very active and busy.

Yet there was an evil leader in the midst of this church corrupting and defiling her. That this woman "Jezebel" calling herself a prophetess, must have had tremendous influence is evident from the letter itself. She was seducing and teaching the same false teaching of the Nicolaitans and she had many who were following her. She was violating the provisions of Acts 15:29. Obviously, her name is not Jezebel but rather she, in her life and influence, is best symbolized by the ancient queen Jezebel who did so much to subvert Israel in the days of Elijah (See 2 Kings 9:22). Moffatt translates, "that Jezebel of a woman." The Lord emphasizes that he had given her warnings before, either through John or some other inspired man. In fact she had had time to repent and she refused. The time of repentance has gone and now the time for judgment has come. Those who are her followers will likewise be subjected to judgment unless they repent of their deeds. Some understand the word "children" to be her spiritual children, while others interpret this as the children of her physical adulteries, like the child of David and Bathsheba. In both the Old and New Testaments, unfaithfulness to God is spoken of in terms of spiritual adultery. The Israelites are accused of going into "harlotry after strange gods" (Ex. 34:15, 16; Deut. 31:16, Ps. 73:27; Hos. 9:1). The New Testament speaks of unfaithful people as "an evil and adulterous generation" (Matt. 12:39; Mark 8:38). In all probability the concept of fornication here is twofold, unfaithfulness to God but also involving physical fornication perhaps. Commentators differ on whether she has gone so far that there is no possibility of any return, or whether this is a preliminary judgment that itself will be a kind of final call to repentance. It would appear from the reading of the text, however, that she has gone beyond the limits of God's patience. Christ, therefore, will help all the churches to know that he understands the feelings and thoughts of every man, and that he knows fully and perfectly each one so that he can judge every man in accordance with his works. One of the important principles set forth in the Scriptures is that God's judgment will be executed in accordance with the deeds or actions of one's life. Obviously, these include the feelings and thoughts that are the mainsprings of one's actions.

Yet Jesus has a message of hope to those who have not defiled themselves with these false teachings, with these so-called "deep things" that really belong to Satan. Apparently the false teachers had talked about the deeper "mysteries" of the faith and referred these to their own particular teachings. The true Christian knows what the real "deep things of God" are and has received them through God's word (1 Cor. 2:10). Christ only calls upon the faithful who remain true to him, to hold fast to his will. Being obedient to the word of God is the important thing. He assures them that they must not be anxious, for he lays upon them no additional burden.

In making his promise to the one who conquers, Christ equates the one "who keeps my works until the end" with "he who conquers," so that we understand what is meant by conquering. He promises to "give him power over the nations and he shall rule them with a rod of iron." The language of this passage agrees with Ps. 2:9, which was regarded as a Messianic Psalm. The word translated "rule" has the meaning of "act as a shepherd," but it is used also in a destructive sense, meaning "to lay waste and devastate," and is undoubtedly used here with that meaning (cf. 12:5; 19:5). Thus the idea is that he shall destroy as with a rod of iron and dash in pieces like vessels of the potter those who fail to follow the Lord. This is another way of saying that the Christian will share in the triumph of the Lord over his enemies, since they must be broken up completely and entirely like the vessels of a potter. In addition, the one who conquers will receive the morning star, which Rev. 22:16 applies to Jesus. The victorious Christian shares in Christ's glorious triumph and authority, and possesses Christ as an everlasting treasure. Whatever may be his inconveniences, difficulties and hardships in this life, he will share in all of the joy and triumph of the victorious Christ. Beginning with this letter, the last four place the exhortation, "He who has an ear, let him hear what the Spirit says to the churches," after the promise to the one who conquers, rather than before the promise as in the first three letters.

Discussion Questions

1. Describe the historical background of the city of Pergamum.

2. What writing material was developed here that was later used in making manuscript copies of the Bible?

3. What pagan religions were centered here?

4. What is meant by "where Satan's throne is"?

5. Review the Old Testament story of Balaam and Balak. What parallels may be drawn from it for the error in the Pergamum church?

6. What pressures were these early Christians subjected to?

7. Can you think of pressures in our modern world to which Christians are subjected today?

8. What various interpretations have been made of the "white stone"?

9. For what was the city of Thyatira most noted?

10. What good and what evil things were pointed out in the Thyatira church?

11. What is the meaning of "Jezebel" here?

12. What meanings are given in the Bible to adultery?

13. Do you think that "Jezebel" had gone beyond the limits of God's patient longsuffering? Is there a time when this can happen to a false teacher or anyone?

14. What is meant by the expression "I will give him power over the nations, and he shall rule them with a rod of iron"?

15. What is the meaning of receiving the morning star?

16. What change of position do you notice in this letter in the expression, "He who has an ear, let him hear what the Spirit says to the churches"?

Lesson 6

THE SEVEN CHURCHES (Part III)
(Revelation 3:1-22)

Letter to Sardis (3:1-6)

This is the letter to the dead Church, with scarcely anything to commend it. Sir William Ramsay points out that Sardis was itself a city of degeneration. Once proud, as the capital of the ancient kingdom of Lydia, it had been feared by the Greeks because its kings sought to rule over the Grecian world. Its name is really a plural noun, for it was the combination of two towns, one in the valley and one on the plateau. Its wealth had been legendary, for its greatest king was Croesus, about whom the proverb was coined, "as rich as Croesus." The Persians conquered this kingdom and incorporated it into their empire. It later came under Roman rule. It had been devastated by an earthquake in A.D. 17, but had been rebuilt through the generosity of Tiberius, the Roman Emperor. Yet it had never achieved its former glory and importance under the Romans.

As is often true, a church becomes very much like its community. You might consider how the community affects the church where you worship. This church was dead, even while it had "the name of being alive." In addressing this church, Christ calls himself the one "who has the seven spirits of God," or the Holy Spirit in all of his gifts and power. He also has the seven stars which, if our interpretation of star as signifying the spiritual aspect of each congregation is correct, is another way of saying that he has his churches spiritually in the palm of his hand. This is a church ready to die (vs. 2). The courtship of the world of Pergamum, the seduction by the world at Thyatira has become at Sardis spiritual death. It is not even interested enough to be troubled about false teaching, nor to be engaged in the struggle. It had little or no opposition because it did not stand for anything. Where the church stands for the truth, there is bound to be opposition to it. The condemnation of this church is severe, and yet there is a small nucleus of faithful members to whom the Lord addresses a word of encouragement. This reminds us that even if we as individuals should be a part of a church that the Lord would describe as dead, if we are faithful and devoted to him, we can still stand in a relationship of life and be among those who overcome. We need not lose heart because we feel the church we attend is spiritually dying.

The appeal to this church is to wake up, to "strengthen what remains" that is about to die, since nothing has been perfect before God. Notice carefully the verb tenses in vs. 3. Once more we come upon these two words: remember and repent. Nothing is so calculated to bring a dying church to life as remembering what it has received from the word of God. If this word is heeded and obeyed, it brings to life again. It makes men come to see their own spiritual condition once more, and with godly grief to repent (2 Cor. 7:10). Failure to wake up, Jesus reminded them, will mean that "I will come like a thief, and you will not know at what hour I will come upon you" (Luke 12:39; Mark 13:32). Very often in the New Testament, the thief is used as a figure of the unexpected coming of Christ (Matt. 24:43; Luke 12:39; 1 Thess. 5:2, 4; 2 Pet. 3:10; Rev. 16:15).

There are a few names (persons) at Sardis whose "garments" (character) are not soiled. Swete thinks that these white garments stand for the new profession that a person made when he was baptized, since at this time all baptism was adult baptism, infant baptism coming in at a later period in church history. They had remained true to Christ and they would share in Christ's fellowship, walking with him in white, similar to the

Twelve who walked with Jesus in his earthly ministry. The meaning of "for they are worthy" (vs. 4) seems here to be, "for they deserve to." While God and Christ are the only ones that are truly worthy, there is a worthiness that comes through faithful living which attaches to the follower of Christ through close fellowship with him.

The one that overcomes will be dressed in white garments. Some have interpreted these as the wedding garments mentioned in Jesus' parable (Matt. 22:11-13). Others have interpreted them as the robes of victory for those who are victorious. While some have referred them to the purity of everlasting life, other commentators have felt that they referred to the resurrection bodies which the faithful would have in the next life. Possibly elements of all these interpretations can be embraced in the figure of white garments, since they are not mutually exclusive. In no wise will their names be rubbed out of the book of life. The term "book of life" occurs several times in the Scriptures (Ex. 32:32, 33; Ps. 69:28; Dan. 12:1; Mal. 3:16; Luke 10:20; Phil. 4:3; Rev. 13:8; 17:8; 20, 15; 21:27). This term refers to the list of those who are God's own people. Christ will acknowledge them before the Father (see Matt. 10:32, 33). Here one of the promises made during Jesus' earthly ministry is repeated.

Letter to Philadelphia (3:7-13)

Philadelphia, founded in the second century B.C., was named after King Attalus II Philadelphus. It was the most recent of the seven cities and had been founded to spread Greek culture and language among the Lydians. It was located some 28 miles southeast of Sardis. This region was subject to earthquakes, and the city was largely destroyed in a great earthquake in A.D. 17; but through the generosity of the emperor it was rebuilt like Sardis. This was a wine-producing region, and we are not surprised to find that the chief pagan cult was the worship of Dionysus, the god of wine. It was probably not a large city, and there is evidence that the church here was small (see vs. 8). Apparently its principal opponents were the Jews, since verse 9 refers to the "synagogue of Satan," a term already used in the letter to Smyrna. There is no mention of persecution by Roman officials, nor opposition from the pagans.

Christ describes himself as the one that is holy and true (vs. 7). This same description is applied to God in 6:10, showing that in Revelation God's attributes are shared with Christ. The word translated "true" (Gr. *alethinos*) means literally "what is genuine or real." He was not a false Christ, but the true one, and the further description points this out. This is largely taken from Isaiah 22:22, and the expression "who has the key of David" was one of the recognized Messianic expressions. Only he can open the door and shut it; only he is able to admit one to the true house of David, the Messianic kingdom. Only he can show the opportunities before the church.

Verse 8 introduces the figure of "an open door," which is used in the New Testament to denote (1) an opportunity for preaching the gospel (1 Cor. 16:9; 2 Cor. 2:12; Col. 4:3), or (2) an admission into a state or place (Rev. 3:20; 4:1). Commentators hold to both points of view. For instance, in keeping with the second meaning, the idea is that the Lord is promising an open door of reward with entrance into his everlasting glory to those who are faithful. In keeping with the first view, others hold that the open door refers to new opportunities of service given to this church. Only Christ has the power to shut the door. The Lord also reminds this church that it has worked, it has a little power, which may refer to its small size and influence in the face of its enemies. It did not deny his name in time of persecution, but kept his word.

Verse 9. Some of the bitterest foes that the church seems to have had were Jews. Twenty years later, Ignatius (*The Epistle to the Philadelphians*, ch. 6) says that one of their great dangers is now from Judaizing Christians. However, at this time the problem is still from outside. Christ states that the day will come when the Jews who have rejected him will come along with all men to acknowledge him, and to know that the church, though hated and despised as a small, persecuted group, is the object of the victorious Lord's love (see Phil. 2:10,11). The Lord promises that because they have been faithful in keeping his word, which encourages them to steadfastness, he will preserve them "from the hour of trial that is coming on the whole world." "Those who dwell upon the earth" is a descriptive term referring to the unbelievers in this book (11:10; 13:8-12,14; 17:8). Just what this hour of trial actually was we cannot say. Some refer it to persecutions; some refer it to the time of judgment which will fall upon the world at the end, looked at in the foreshortened view of the prophet. The type of protection referred to in the sealing of the 144,000 in chapter 7 may be in view. Because Christ is the one that comes, his encouragement to them is to hold fast that no one should take away their crown. The word "crown" (Gr. *stephanos*) is thought of in the context of winning the game rather than of someone stealing a treasure. Christ's promise to come quickly is simply another way of emphasizing the fact that we must be constantly expectant and watchful. As the faithful leaders on earth could be called "pillars" of the church (Gal. 2:9), so faithful ones can become pillars in the sanctuary of glory. They will be inscribed with the name of God and God's city, "the New Jerusalem which comes down from my God out of heaven," a proleptic reference that will be explained later in this book (see 21:2). Christ's new name is his name in glory which Christ writes on the one who conquers. The promises made to this church are striking in number, as if to reassure and encourage them in their difficult position.

Letter to Laodicea (3:14-22)

Laodicea was located about 40 miles southeast of Philadelphia, where the great road from Sardis reached the Lycus River Valley. It was named by Antiochus, king of Syria, its founder, after his wife Laodice, and was located about 10 miles west of Colossae. In this same valley the city of Hierapolis was situated (Col. 4:13). Laodicea had flourished under Roman rule, and became a great banking center with considerable wealth. Even though it was severely damaged in the earthquake of A.D. 61, it arose from its ruins without having to accept an imperial subsidy. It was also famous as a center for the manufacture of woolen goods, and as a medical center with a flourishing medical school. The expressions "poor, blind, and naked" refer to the chief commercial and professional activities of the city. The church was founded by Epaphras from Colossae (Col. 1:7; 4:12ff) and Paul had addressed a letter to them (Col. 4:16) which has been lost, unless the Ephesian letter, which may have been a circular letter, is this letter. The church seems to have gained quite a number of those who were wealthy, and can be described as a rich church. No word of commendation is given to it. Christ addresses himself to them as the God of truth, the Amen, a title that is reserved to God in Isaiah 65:16 (RSV). This guarantees the truth of what he says. This and the other titles are drawn from 1:5,6. As the faithful and true witness, who sealed his testimony of truth with the giving of his life's blood, he is the beginning of the creation of God, a term that reminds us of Colossians 1:15,18. The New English Bible renders the expression "the beginning of the creation of God" more accurately as "the prime source of all God's creation." Christ is the creator, not a part of the creation.

Christ describes this church by the famous term "lukewarm." This is neither a totally indifferent church nor a fervent church, but is proud and complacent. It feels that it needs nothing. Christ expresses the wish, "Would you were cold or hot!" The Lord does not want men to be neutral and indifferent. One of the great difficulties the church has always faced is the problem of the lack of concern on the part of many who claim to wear the name of Christ. It just does not matter to them. Christ finds this church nauseating to him, and his threat is to spew them out. This is an extremely strong expression. Verses 17,18 explain the complacency of this church. Boastingly, it feels secure in its wealth. It feels it has won all its spiritual wealth. Yet in the sight of Christ it is a wretched church, pitiable and poor and blind and naked. In this city in which wealth and fine woolen cloth and the famous Phrygian powder for eye salve characterize the life of the city, it is interesting that their church should be described in terms of these three major enterprises. Christ advises this church to

55

quit trusting in its own riches, but to buy from him the true gold, the true covering, the true medicine (cf. Isa. 55:1). The true riches is the gold tested in the fire, which means a new understanding of what true riches involves. White garments emphasize the cleansed and perfect character through being washed in the Lamb's blood. The open eyes to see one's own true condition and to see clearly God's way come about only as eye salve will make the eyes once more to see. This has been a harsh rebuke, yet verse 19 reminds the church that the Lord expresses his love in his reproofs and chastenings. To have faults pointed out, to see one's failures in all of their stark reality is not an expression of the Lord's authority so much as of his love. The call is to be zealous, fervent, on fire. (Note that this is a present imperative, in Greek expressing continuing action—keep on being zealous.) The Lord demands their repentance.

Verse 20. In beautiful imagery, Christ is pictured as standing at the door and knocking. Apparently, this refers to each individual at whose door he calls and knocks, inviting any man to hear and open the door that Christ may come into his life and hold close fellowship at the table of his own heart. For the Oriental, fellowship in a meal in the home is one of the greatest expressions of true love and confidence. Christ promises this for us if we will open the door and allow him to come into our lives. In making the great promise, he says that as he has shared in the throne of God, so those who are faithful to him will share in the glory and triumph of his victory. Thus our lives are hid with Christ in God (Col. 3:3). On this glorious note the letters to the seven churches come to an end. Thus one section of the book is completed and the next chapter introduces an entirely new one.

Discussion Questions

1. In what ways does the city of Sardis resemble the church at Sardis?

2. In what way was the Sardis church worse than the church at Pergamum or the church at Thyatira?

3. What lesson does the little nucleus of faithful members at Sardis teach us?

4. What can we as individuals do to keep the church from dying spiritually?

5. What admonition did Christ give to this church to bring it to life again spiritually?

6. Discuss the passages in the New Testament where Christ's coming is compared to the unexpected coming of the thief.

7. What interpretations have been given to the white garments the faithful receive?

8. Describe the history and importance of Philadelphia.

9. What is the background and meaning of the term "the key of David"?

10. Discuss the figure of the open door.

11. What problems for the church at Philadelphia were created by the Jews?

12. What meaning is given throughout Revelation to the expression "those who dwell on the earth"?

13. What interpretations have been given to the expression "the hour of trial" in chapter 3:10?

14. What promises are made in the letter to the Philadelphians to the one who overcomes?

15. Give the history of Laodicea.

16. How would you describe a "lukewarm" church today?

17. To what major enterprises of Laodicea does Christ relate his exhortation to this church?

18. How can one understand the love of Christ in the sharp rebuke Christ gives the Laodicean church?

19. Discuss the imagery and meaning of chapter 3:20.

Lesson 7

THE THRONE SCENE (Part III)
(Revelation 4:1-11)

Introduction

It is clear that with the beginning of this chapter one passes into another part of Revelation. As chapters two and three with their short letters are related to the opening vision and concern themselves with the church and its struggles on earth, chapter four pictures to us God on his throne, with the spiritual beings surrounding him, and the adoration of the heavenly hosts in worship to God. The exalted expressions of worship, with their beautiful poetical reminders of Old Testament adorations, lift one above the struggles, discouragements, and strife of the church in the world. To see God as sovereign on his throne ruling in his universe must have been of tremendous encouragement to the scattered, struggling Christians at the close of the first century.

An Open Door (4:1)

"After this I looked." This phrase occurs in 7:9; 15:5; 18:1; while similar expressions occur in 5:1,2,6,11. The expression "and I saw" occurs in each of the remaining chapters of the book except 11 and 12.

The prophet sees a door opened in heaven. This is a door through which he would be able to look in and behold the heavenly scene and the heavenly court. Previous lessons have shown us that the figure of an open door is not new in the Scriptures. Christ had set an open door before the church at Philadelphia (3:8), and he called for an open door in the letter to Laodicea (3:20). Yet the word "open" implies that the door has already been opened and stands ready for him to come in. Then the clear call comes to the prophet, apparently the same voice that addressed him in such trumpet-like tones in chapter 1:10. There it was the Lord who gave him his commission. Here it is this same trumpet-like voice that calls him up to the door that he might be shown "what must take place after this." To raise the question as to how Christ could call him when later in the vision he appears as the Lamb before the throne overlooks the fact that these visions are filled with symbolic elements. It is the voice of Christ that calls, not the form of Christ that appears here.

The Throne of God (4:2,3)

Immediately the prophet is in the Spirit's power and is caught up to see this view in heaven. Some scholars have tried to see this as a higher degree of the Spirit's power than in chapter 1:10, but the expressions are identical. Apparently he remains here until the close of chapter 9. For instance, passages like chapter 5:4,5 in which one of the elders speaks to him, chapter 6:9 in which he sees underneath the altar the souls of those that had been slain for the world of God and the testimony of Jesus Christ, chapter 7:13,14 in which one of the elders asks him the question rhetorically about who are the ones around the throne that are arrayed in the white robes—all indicate that he is still in heaven. In fact, as one goes through the remaining visions of the book, part of these visions occur from the aspect of heaven, and part of them from the viewpoint of the earth.

The first thing he saw was a throne and the One who sits upon it dominates the whole scene. No endeavor is made to describe the One who sits upon the throne in terms that are personal, but simply in terms of precious gems flashing their brilliance. This is a vast throne room, and the central point of interest is the One who sits upon the throne. The expression "seated on the throne" refers to reigning power or dominion over a kingdom. In his great sovereignty God rules over the whole universe. The emphasis in this expression is not upon his resting upon his throne but rather upon his reigning on the throne. Commentators have referred to chapters four and five as "the throne scene," since the term "throne" occurs 19 times in its singular and plural uses. In the Old Testament God's throne is referred to more than once (1 Kings 22:19; Ps. 47:8; Isa. 6:1; Ezek. 1:26; Dan. 7:9). In most of the chapters of Revelation mention is made of the throne of God.

Three precious gems are used in verse 3 to describe God rather than any human shapes or forms. Commentators differ in trying to identify these stones. Some identify the jasper with the diamond while others identify it as the opal. The Greek word can also refer to a dull opaque stone or to a colored stone. The carnelian is usually identified as a red-colored stone while the emerald may be like the color of our modern emerald. Other authorities identify the word translated "emerald" as a colorless rock crystal that is capable of reflecting rainbow hues. The rainbow was a sign in the Old Testament of the covenant that God had made with his people not to destroy them by water (see Gen. 9:11-16). Some see this as a token of God as a covenant-making God, while others see it only as a symbol of his splendor. Whatever may be the meaning of the bow, it concealed the glorious person of God from the eyes of the prophet. Any effort to try to identify the meaning of these colors with aspects of God's nature can only be highly tentative and we shall not make the attempt.

Twenty-Four Thrones

About the throne is the circle of 24 thrones, with 24 elders arrayed in white garments and wearing golden crowns (Gr. *stephanoi*) upon their heads. Two Greek words are used in Revelation for crown. The one used here refers to the wreath of victory which the winners in athletic contests received to make their triumph. The crowns here signify a victorious consummation for the 24 elders. As we look further in the book, we note that these elders who sit around the throne cast their crowns before the throne (4:10) and worship the one who sits upon the throne (4:11; 5:11,12,14; 11:16; 19:4). One of them encourages the weeping prophet (5:5) and one of them interprets the meaning of one of the visions (7:13,14). What interpretations have been given to the 24 elders? Interpreters have referred to them as a heavenly court or council over which God rules, and they are thought to be a kind of college of angels or heavenly creatures. Other scholars have seen them as the angelic representatives of the 24 orders of priests which are described in 1 Chronicles 24:7-18. These are the ones who stand and offer to God the prayers of the faithful and thus represent the perfect heavenly worship as archetypes of the temple and its worship. However, others have seen the 24 as representing God's people, 12 from the Old Testament, possibly symbolic of the 12 tribes with the 12 patriarchs associated with them, and 12 for the New Covenant people (the church), possibly represented by the 12 apostles. The idea here would be that the elders represent God's people under covenant, whether the Old or New Covenant people. A variation of this view looks upon the elders as heavenly representatives of all the faithful, particularly as a royal priesthood offering worship and service to God (see 1:6). The last view seems more likely to this writer.

Four Living Creatures (4:5-8a)

Lightnings, voices, and thunders proceed from God's throne, expressive of his majesty and power. Before the throne there are seven lamps of fire burning steadily. These are interpreted to be the seven spirits of God. This same expression is found in 1:4, descriptive of the Holy Spirit in his full sanctifying, enlightening, and revealing power. Just as in Ex. 19:16ff God's presence had expressed itself in his meeting with the children of Israel at Mount Sinai in lightnings, thunders, and loud voices, so here God's throne in majesty and glory expresses the presence of God. Stretching out before the throne is a great expanse, a pavement "as it were," a sea of crystal clear glass, flashing back the light that falls upon it, perhaps like a sea reflecting the sunlight. Yet there is nothing in human experience quite like it, so he uses the expression "as it were." Perhaps there is expressed in this a sort of parallel to the laver of the old tabernacle, just as the seven flaming lamps remind one of the seven-branch candlestick that stood in the tabernacle. This brilliant pavement suggests the glory of God as well as the separation that existed between John and the glorious throne of God. The prophet did not come close to the throne, but he saw it across the sea resembling glass.

Verse 6. The expression "on each side of the throne" can probably be best understood as meaning in the middle of each of the four sides and yet between the throne and a larger circle made by the 24 thrones. The four living creatures are covered with eyes. A close parallel exists here between these living creatures and those described in Ezekiel 1. The creatures in Ezekiel are the bearers of the throne, and each has four faces—the face of a man, a lion, an ox, and an eagle—while here each creature has his own characteristic face. The order is different in Ezekiel 1 and Revelation 4, but the same creatures are mentioned. The early church fathers used these symbols as representative of the four gospel writers, assigning to each one a symbol. Not all agree on these symbols. Many interpret these as the cherubim that support the throne of God. Some think they personify attributes of God. Many commentators think they represent the whole animate creation as it praises and adores God, while others think they simply represent the highest order of angels in the heavenly court. This writer inclines to the latter view. Their wings indicate their swiftness, while their being full of eyes indicates their sleepless vigilance. They join in offering praise and adoration in one of the beautiful hymns preserved in this part of the book (vs. 8).

Heavenly Hymns (4:8b-11)

This first hymn reminds us of the great hymn found in Isaiah 6. The theme of their hymn is praise and adoration to God. Here God is described as the Lord, and as the Almighty whose sovereignty and power are over all the universe. He is also described as the One "who was and is and is to come" which emphasizes his eternity. The distinctive character of the Old Testament revelation of God is that he is a holy God. The central meaning of holiness is otherness or separation from the limited, finite, creaturely, and sinful. The secondary meaning of holiness has to do with God's absolute purity. This hymn also reminds us of the way in which the book opens in its declaration of God (1:8).

The elders join the living creatures in their worship and thanksgiving to the One who sits upon the throne and lives forever, falling down and prostrating themselves before him and casting their crowns before the throne. Some interpreters see here symbolized the fact that God's people join the whole universe in praising and giving God glory. Others see here merely the symbolism of the whole order of the heavenly court praising and glorifying God. One does not need to think that the elders are always prostrate, but that there are occasions where they join in the worship of God as they praise and honor him (see 5:8; 11:16; 19:4). Their crowns are cast before him because no crown can stand before the authority of God, and their crowns of victory are rewards to them from a God whose rule is supreme. God has enabled them to overcome and enjoy the victory.

The second hymn is a hymn of praise to God as worthy to receive the adoration of men because he is the creator, and all things come from him and depend upon him. God's glory is shown in his mighty works. His creation makes manifest his own glory (Ps. 8; 19:1-6; Rom. 1:18-20). It is the 24 elders who express their praise of God because "thou didst create all things." How much more is the Lord of all glory worthy of being called "our Lord and our God" than the Roman Emperor Domitian who makes the claim to be "Dominus (Lord) et Deus (God)"? God's people, through their heavenly representatives (the 24 elders), join the heavenly host in praising God for his creative work.

Conclusion

This lesson has moved us from the earth with its troubles, struggles, and sin through the open door to the perfect peace and purity of heaven. The scene of the throne of God and the heavenly court around the throne adoring and proclaiming his holiness has occupied the major portion of this chapter. The emphasis in chapter four is on his creatorship of the world and all that is in it. For this he is praised and adored by the heavenly hosts. The next lesson will focus attention upon God's great provisions for human redemption, and we shall witness the praise of the heavenly hosts for his gracious provisions.

Discussion Questions

1. What contrast is drawn between the materials of chapters two and three and those of chapter four in the introductory comments to this lesson?

2. What significance attaches to the expressions "after this I looked" and "and I saw"?

3. How is the figure of the open door used elsewhere in the Scriptures?

4. Discuss what is meant by the prophet being "in the Spirit."

5. How can we tell whether the prophet views his visions from earth or from heaven?

6. How is God described in this vision?

7. On what basis have chapters four and five been called by scholars "the throne scene"?

8. What significance do you see in the Greek words that are used for crown in the Book of Revelation?

9. Discuss the interpretations given of the 24 elders. Which interpretation do you think is the most likely?

10. After reading Ezekiel 1, what similarities and what differences do you see between the creatures described there and the living creatures?

11. What interpretations have been given of the four living creatures here?

12. What is the meaning of "holiness" as it is applied to God? How is God's holiness set forth in this first great hymn?

13. What is the emphasis in the second hymn? Who joins in this hymn?

14. What titles were claimed by the Roman emperor? Do you see any contrast here to the hymn of praise given to God?

Lesson 8

THE LAMB AND THE SEALED BOOK
(Revelation 5:1-14)

Introduction

After witnessing this beautiful scene that lifts up our hearts in worship, the prophet calls us once more to look at the throne. In this chapter the slain Lamb is introduced and receives all the worship, adoration, and acclaim that God, who sits on the throne, received in chapter 4. The whole heavenly court, all the orders of spiritual beings, and the creatures in all the universe join in giving to both God and the slain Lamb (Christ) the same worship.

The Closely Sealed Book (5:1-3)

John sees "a scroll" (book) in the right hand of the One who sits on the throne. This book is written on the inside and on the outside as well. This is an unusual thing because scrolls in the ancient world were written on only one side. Also in Ezekiel the prophet saw a roll opened out before him written on the front and on the back with a message of lamentations, mourning, and woe (Ezek. 2:10). The book John saw was a sort of book of destiny for the universe that will be unfolded by the Lord and given to his people through John. The RSV describes it as "sealed with seven seals." The perfect participle with the compound verb in Greek used here emphasizes an intensive force, so that it is so closely sealed that only divine power can open and make it known. Some have tried to use a will in Roman law that bore seven seals of seven witnesses secured by threads in the parchment as a parallel to this as a will or testament relating to the Old Testament or the New Testament. However, if this is the analogy that is in mind, then the testament could not be executed until all the seals were broken, including the seventh seal. Yet here the seals are also a part of the message. In the breaking of the seals, and the consequent sounding of the trumpets that occupy the visions of the remainder of the first half of the book through chapter 11, there are aspects of the will being carried out. Therefore, this will is the will of God, not a particular testament as we might know it. We recall that at the beginning of this vision the promise of the Lord was to "show you what must take place after this" (4:1). There is no mention of anyone actually reading the book, even after the seals are broken. Each seal being broken adds to the picture. This closely sealed book is not a book that is read aloud but a book that is enacted upon the stage of history. This knowledge can only come through one who is able to break the seals, open the book and reveal the things that are to come.

Next the prophet sees a strong angel, no doubt called strong because of the loud voice with which he announces to the whole universe his challenge. "Who is worthy to open the scroll and break its seals?" Obviously this book could not be opened until the seals were broken. This is an expression in which the ability to open the book is the first and most important thing, and therefore takes first place in the order of thought, even though breaking the seals comes chronologically before the opening of the book. No one in the whole universe is able to answer this challenge, whether in heaven, on the earth, or under the earth. This threefold division of the universe reminds us of the statement made by Paul concerning the three regions that shall acknowledge Christ above all (Phil. 2:10).

The Prophet Wept (5:4,5)

Because of this unmet challenge, the prophet wept bountifully, since "no one was found worthy" (had the rank and position and, therefore, ability to open the book). No one was able to look in and, therefore, the whole matter of revelation came to a halt here. This is a dramatic touch, since God knew who would be able to open the book and reveal what was to come. He did not have to search through the universe to find Christ. The answer that follows lets us know this. Yet the incident emphasizes the dramatic quality of this book.

One of the elders stops John's weeping. If our interpretation of the elders is correct, one of those who have experienced redemption calls upon the prophet to stop his weeping. There is One who is able to open the book, One who has conquered. The negative present imperative in Greek translated "weep not" has the force of commanding one to stop what he has started to do. It is located in the emphatic position in this verse. The one described as "the Lion of the tribe of Judah, the Root of David," has won the victory that gives him the right to open the book by breaking its seven seals. This title goes back to two Old Testament passages (Gen. 49:9 and Isa. 11:1). The noblest son of the tribe was called "the Lion of the tribe" in Old Testament times. The "Lion of the tribe of Judah" would then be the outstanding member of the tribe of Judah. Genesis 49:9 was interpreted Messianically at this time by the Jews, and Isaiah 11:1-10 was likewise applied by Jews to the Messiah before the birth of Christ. Jesus Christ came of the line of David, (Matt. 1:1-16) of the tribe of Judah. The meaning of the expression "Root of David" is that the Messiah would come from the line of David. Swete comments, "As the prophet foresaw, the stump of the old tree of the house of David had sent forth a new David to rule the nations" (*The Apocalypse of St. John*, p. 77). This is repeated in chapter 22:16. Christ thus fulfills the Messianic promises of the Old Testament which is what the apostolic preaching had affirmed (Acts 2:30,34,35; 3:24 and others).

The Lamb Took the Scroll (5:6,7)

Although one looks for the Lion, it is a Lamb that takes the center of attention in the vision. Between the throne, with its inner circle of four living creatures and among its larger circle

69

of the elders, a Lamb is standing. Twenty-nine times in twelve chapters of this book, Christ is called the Lamb. He is often described as a Lamb elsewhere in the New Testament (John 1:29,36; Acts 8:32ff [Isa. 53:7]; 1 Pet. 1:19).

The twofold designation of Christ as Lion and Lamb emphasizes the unique combination of conqueror and sacrifice. He is "a Lamb standing, as though it had been slain," still bearing the marks of his wounds upon him. He had been slain, but was now living. One is reminded here of the risen Christ who showed his disciples his wounds (John 20:20,27). The Greek word translated "slain" in reference to Christ's death is used a number of times in this book and calls to mind the words of the Greek translation of the Old Testament for Isaiah 53:7 in reference to the lamb led to slaughter. This word carries with it the idea of a slain sacrifice. The Lamb is introduced here as the great sacrifice for our sins—the One who by this sacrifice can be said to have conquered, and who can claim for himself all others who will share in his victory as those who conquer. In the background of this picture is the great prophetic passage from Isaiah 53, "He was brought as a lamb to the slaughter and as a sheep before her shearers is dumb so he openeth not his mouth" (Isa. 53:7, KJV). The term "standing" is interpreted by some scholars as symbolizing the fact that his life is restored and his sacrifice is accepted. Others interpret this to mean that he is "ready for action." Possibly both ideas are involved, since they do not exclude one another.

He has seven horns and seven eyes. In the Old Testament, the horn was the symbol of strength and power (Deut. 33:17); also it symbolized honor and royal dignity (Ps. 89:17). The Lamb with seven horns is the all-powerful king of righteousness. He may be contrasted with the seven-headed beast with ten horns who will be the agent of the dragon described in chapter 13:1. The seven eyes symbolize the fullness of his vision, by which he knows all and sees all things. Nothing escapes his vision. In the vision in chapter 1, his eyes are described as flaming fire, while here they are identified as the seven spirits of God, now sent forth into the world. The victorious Lamb, having triumphed over death, sent the Holy Spirit forth into the world as his own Spirit. This is what was promised in John 14:26 and other passages dealing with the coming of the Holy Spirit. After his resurrection he breathed upon the disciples and said, "Receive the Holy Spirit" (John 20:22). No contradiction should be seen between the seven eyes of the Lamb, as the seven spirits of God sent forth into all the world, and the seven spirits of God, as the seven candlesticks before God's throne. Here the eyes are on a mission for the Lamb. They are sent forth to exhibit the presence of Christ with his people in the Holy Spirit. Zechariah had spoken of the eyes of the Lord "which run to and fro through the whole earth" (Zech. 4:10).

The verbs are interesting in this passage. After saying, "he went," the perfect tense is used in Greek "has taken," since the perfect tense describes an action in the past that has permanent results flowing from it. Christ receives this book as an abiding possession. In taking this book, Christ is able to unfold the future and make known the ultimate consummation of God's purposes. Later in the book (22:1) the throne is called "the throne of God and of the Lamb" because it is a throne shared by Christ with God. God rules the world through Christ. This has already been stated in a different way in 3:21.

Hymns in Heaven (5:8-14)

This section introduces us to three great hymns or songs which express the praise of the heavenly court and all of God's creatures because God's great purpose for redeeming man has been made known through Jesus Christ. The first hymn is the hymn of the four living creatures and the four and twenty elders offering to the Lamb the same worship that they have offered to the One who sits upon the throne. Each one of them holds a harp and "golden bowls full of incense, which are the prayers of the saints." The KJV reads, "golden vials, full of odours," since it uses the word "vial" for bowl. Obviously, both the harp, an instrument of joyful music, and the golden bowls full of incense are symbolic. Swete points this out in

71

saying, "The prayers of the church are symbolized by the incense as its psalmody, already an important element in church worship (1 Cor. 14:15,26; Eph. 5:19; Col 3:16), is represented by the lyres" (*The Apocalypse of St. John*, p. 80). Swete goes on to say that the use of literal incense in a ceremonial way in the services of the church does not have any support in the period before Nicea (A.D. 325), although the later church made it a necessary accompaniment of the celebration of the Lord's supper. The introduction of incense and instrumental music in the worship of the church on earth came centuries after the New Testament. No case can be made for either incense or instrumental music in Christian worship from these symbolic references. "The prayers of the saints" refer to the prayers of those who are the Lord's holy ones on earth. Note that "saints" in the Scriptures do not refer to some special class, but rather refer to the church on earth (Rom. 1:7; 15:25,26; 16:2,15; 1 Cor. 1:2; Phil. 1:1 and others). Saints are simply Christians, persons set apart for God's service, offering to him prayers here symbolized as incense after the type of the worship at the tabernacle and temple under Judaism. The later meaning of "saint" as some dead hero who has been so recognized through an elaborate ecclesiastical ceremony known as canonization came many centuries after the New Testament period.

The song is called "a new song" because it has a new theme, the redemption through Christ. The new song is a part of a number of things described as "new" in the book: the new name (2:17; 3:12), the new Jerusalem (3:12; 21:2), the new heaven and the new earth (21:1), all things new (21:5). The word translated "new" emphasizes that it is something different from anything that has ever been, and therefore is new in quality. The emphasis in this song is upon Christ's great sacrificial death by which men are redeemed. He is "worthy" not because of his perfect life on earth, nor of his unique relationship to God as his Son (although these are all true), but because of the greatness of his sacrifice, "for (Gr. *hoti*, "because") thou wast slain." Through being slain on the cross he purchased with the currency of his blood men from every tribe, tongue, people, and nation. He purchased them for God (1 Cor. 6:20; 7:23; 2 Pet.

2:1). The power of Jesus' death releases us from the hostile power of evil and Satan. The fact that Jesus' death reached beyond the limits of fleshly Israel to include all men is forcefully emphasized in this great hymn. The power of his redeeming blood has made the redeemed people "a kingdom and priests to our God." The universal priesthood of all Christians is one of the important teachings in the New Testament. Under the Mosaic law a priest was the only one who could enter into the holy place. Every man had to offer his sacrifice and bring his worship to God through the priest. In the New Testament the priests are Christians, for priests are those who have the right to approach God. Boldly, as Christians, we may approach the throne of God to offer worship and adoration, because the redeeming blood of Christ has made this possible for us. Through Jesus Christ, "they shall reign on the earth." The KJV reads here "and hath made us unto our God kings and priests: and we shall reign on the earth," following a different manuscript tradition, but the meaning practically is the same. Because he has triumphed, they also live triumphantly. No reference is made here to a political sovereignty, nor to a millennial reign on earth, but rather to a spiritual ruling that they share with Jesus Christ.

The second hymn arises from the vast number of angels around the throne and the circle of the living creatures and the circle of the elders. With a loud voice they call out their praise. The sevenfold ascription of praise is given to the Lamb. The Lamb that was slain deserves "to receive power and wealth and wisdom and might and honor and glory and blessing." All the honor, glory, and blessing of the whole universe he deserves to receive because of the redemption he has provided. Because he emptied himself and subjected himself to the shameful death of the cross, he has been exalted above all and given a name above every name (Phil. 2:5ff). Thus everything that has been said concerning God in 4:11 is now said concerning Christ.

The third hymn addresses both God and Christ together and offers blessing, honor, glory, and might. To each one of these is added the definite article "the" for emphasis in the Greek. As chapter 4 had concentrated on God and the creation, chapter 5 concentrates on Christ and his redemption, climaxing in the last two verses to join both together in receiving adoration and worship. The whole creation joins in this final hymn. All creatures of sky, earth, and sea, and the realm of Hades below join in this great doxology. The four living creatures keep on saying, "amen," since the imperfect tense in the Greek used here expresses the continuing action in past time. The elders prostrate themselves before God and Christ and worship.

Conclusion

This lesson has been a commentary on the opening verse of the Book of Revelation, for it has shown to us the worthiness and authority of the slain Lamb of God, Jesus Christ, to make this revelation of God's purposes and their ultimate consummation in triumphant victory. Who is worthy but the one who gave his life that men might be redeemed and through his shed blood overcame evil? He takes the book and is able to break the seals. He is the revealer. To him the whole hosts of heaven give adoration and praise and join their worship of God with their worship of the Lamb. Unmistakably, all whom God receives the Lamb also receives, and the prayer of John 17:5 is answered.

Discussion Questions

1. Why does the book, written inside and outside and sealed down, interest John so much?

2. What is the force of the expression, "sealed"?

3. Why do you suppose the strong angel made his challenge to the whole universe?

4. What is meant by saying, "No one was found worthy"?

5. What is the significance of the expression "the Lion that is of the tribe of Judah, the Root of David"?

6. What other passages in the New Testament can you find that will emphasize that Christ came from the line of David?

7. How can Christ be both a Lion and a Lamb?

8. What Old Testament prophecy is referred to in speaking of Christ as a Lamb "slain"?

9. What does the horn symbolize, and what do the seven eyes symbolize? What difference is there between the way that the Holy Spirit is pictured in chapter four and in this chapter?

10. How are we to understand the harps and golden bowls full of incense in this passage?

11. What use is sometimes made of this passage to justify instrumental music in worship today, and what would you say about this?

12. When were incense and instrumental music introduced into worship after the New Testament?

13. Discuss the meaning of "saint" in the New Testament.

14. What had Christ by his death accomplished?

15. Who join in the hymns ascribing praise to the Lamb?

Lesson 9

THE SIX SEALS
(Revelation 6:1-17)

Introduction

After the Lamb had received the book sealed with the seven seals, there followed the breaking of the seals. This lesson concerns the breaking of the first six seals and what happens in connection with each one.

From this point in the Book of Revelation commentators have differed widely in their interpretations of its symbols. Following the basic point of view outlined in the second lesson of this series, each group of interpreters has looked upon the symbols that follow according to his own basic position. Some have referred these entirely to events in the future, connecting them with the seven-year "rapture" which they believe immediately precedes the millennium on earth. Others have tried to pattern these as a part of an unfolding, continuous historical scheme, identifying each one with some specific historic event. For instance, Barnes in his *Notes* interprets the first seal as beginning with A.D. 96, the close of the reign of Domitian, and lasting for several years. The other seals he blocks out through the second, third, and fourth centuries in succession, interpreting the sixth seal as the invasion of the Roman Empire by the barbarians. He makes the trumpets to continue this historical pattern of invasions up through the conquest of Constantinople by the Turks (A.D. 1453). This makes the Book of Revelation describe in detail a continuous historical pattern.

Other commentators interpret the seals entirely within the contemporary scene of John's day.

From our viewpoint, however, the Book of Revelation does not purport to give such a detailed forecast of Western European history. It is not to be identified with any specific events or persons. Although some correspondences can be found between events that took place in the early centuries, this is not its primary meaning. It is much more symbolic of the woes and frustrations that will characterize the things "which must come hereafter." The first four seals comprise a series. Each seal is preceded by a call from one of the four living creatures and introduces a horse and rider. A parallel may be found in the vision of Zechariah 6:1-8 where four groups of horses and chariots bearing similar colors to these horses in Revelation are described. The order of their appearance is different as is probably also the purpose of the horses.

The wording followed in the King James Version would lead one to think that this is an invitation to John to "come and see." However, the KJV here follows late manuscript evidence, and the RSV follows earlier and better manuscript evidence. Following the series of the four horses and horsemen, the fifth seal shows the martyrs who had given their lives for the faith, while the sixth seal points to the earth-shaking events before the "great day of their wrath."

The First Four Seals (6:1-8)

John looks when the Lamb opens the first of the seven seals, and he hears the commanding voice of the first of the four living creatures saying, "Come!" This command is addressed to each one of the four horsemen by the living creatures, not to John nor to Christ. The first horse is white, and the rider has a bow and is given a crown; and as he goes forth he is "conquering and to conquer."

What does the white horse symbolize? The white horse among the ancients symbolized victory. A number of commentators, under the influence of chapter 19:11ff, refer the white horse to Christ or to the conquering force of the gospel itself. While this may be true, a look at the other three horsemen in this series shows that they are associated not with the gospel, but with the forces of men who are trying to live without God. The only similarity between this horse and rider and the horsemen described in 19:11ff is the color of the horse. The crown worn by this rider is the crown of the victor (Gr. *stephanos*), while the many crowns worn by the rider in chapter 19:12 are diadems (Gr. *diademata*), the royal crowns. In the light of the context, a great number of commentators understand this conquering horse to symbolize conquering warfare, the victorious militarism that has characterized the imperialistic nations and rulers down through the centuries. The bow stands for military power (Jer. 51:56; Ps. 46:9), the aggressive weapon of attack against other peoples. This could refer not only to Rome's imperialism, or the Parthian empire, Rome's great eastern rival, but to any imperialism down through the ages to our modern day.

At the opening of the second seal and the command "come" the "bright red horse" whose rider is given the privilege of taking "peace from the earth" with his great sword, the sword of battle, rides forth and men slay one another. Following upon the heels of conquest and imperialism is international strife and civil strife, the latter particularly stirred up through the jealousies and animosities of selfish men. Surely the bright red horse underlines the slaughter that comes through war. Some have limited the meaning of this horse and its rider simply to the slaughter that accompanies warfare.

With the breaking of the third seal, a black horse comes in view. The rider has "a balance in his hand" and the voice that describes the situation coming from the midst of the four living creatures indicates famine, scarcity, and want. The purpose of this voice is not to alleviate the scarcity, but to show the extent of it. The prices given indicate the difficulty the poor will experience. Barley was the grain of the poor man from which he made his dark colored bread, while wheat was more expensive. The measure (Gr. *choinix*) contained about a quart according to Herodotus, the daily consumption of a man. The Roman coin, "denarius," was the daily wage of a laborer. Thus the day laborer by working all day could buy about a quart of wheat, just enough bread for himself, or about three quarts of barley, just enough for himself, his wife, and family. It was all the worker could do to simply feed himself with nothing left over for shelter, clothing, or the other needs of life. This is a picture of near starvation. This is the picture of scarcity and want that rides in the wake of imperialistic militarism, warfare and civil strife. The prices indicate extreme inflation since ordinarily a denarius would buy from 8 to 12 times this much. Because in times of scarcity the poor suffer more than the rich, the oil and wine would not be hurt. Grain, oil, and wine were the principal crops of Palestine and became the symbols in the Old Testament for the fruits of the earth. The rich would have their oil and wine, but the scarcity would hurt the poor laborers more. In times of dislocation, one need not posit the rebellion of nature itself in order to have conditions of famine and want. The upheavals resulting from warfare and strife along with a social order that fails to distribute equitably the goods at hand can produce such a situation. One does not need to look for some reference to any specific famine in history here. This is reenacted again and again in the world's history.

The fourth seal introduces the "pale horse" with a deathly color, ridden by Death, with Hades following him. Death is here personified. Hades is simply the realm of the dead, also personified, and to these two is given "power over a fourth of the earth, to kill with sword and with famine and with pestilence and by wild beasts of the earth." Four specific types of calamitous death, reminiscent of judgments of God upon disobedient men in the Old Testament, are specified (Ezek. 14:21). The fraction, "a fourth," indicates that this is not complete or absolute and not a reference to the final destruction. Hades always follows death because it gathers in the souls of those who have their exit through death. Bowman has called these first four seals "the sad story of man's frustrations and the futility of his labors; it is the cyclic rumble of the rise and fall of cultures and civilizations" (*The Drama of the Book of Revelation*, p. 49). In this book of the fulfillment of God's purposes in history we are not surprised to see these four horsemen often riding in history. This is the story of man endeavoring to make his own way apart from God and in rebellion to his will. The first four seals belong together.

The Fifth Seal (6:9-11)

The scene changes radically, and John sees underneath the heavenly altar the souls of the martyrs, those "slain for the word of God and for the witness they had borne." The altar calls to mind the brazen altar of sacrifice in the old tabernacle and the later temple, at the foot of which the blood of victims was poured out (Lev. 4:7). At the base of the old brazen altar, the blood, the life, was sacrificed (Lev. 17:11). Here the souls of the martyrs are under the altar because they have been sacrificed, their lifeblood poured out (2 Tim. 4:6). The New Testament emphasizes that each one of us can be a living sacrifice (Rom. 12:1) but these had been called upon to lay down their lives for the Lord and his way. Others like John had been called upon to suffer for a similar reason (cf. 1:9). They cry out for justice and vindication of a righteous God upon a rebellious and God-forgetful world. The expression "those who dwell upon the earth," the earthdwellers, throughout the book refers to those who are not God's people. Throughout the Scriptures God is represented as the one to whom vengeance belongs. "I will repay, says the Lord" (Rom. 12:19). Some find the cry for vindication incongruous with the Christian spirit, pointing out that Jesus prayed for his enemies. However, this parallels Jesus' teaching in Luke 18:7, where the living elect pray to God to vindicate them in the future, while these who have already been sacrificed pray that they may be righteously vindicated in the moral justice of God and his universe. This is not so much a matter of personal vindication as it is for the bringing of his justice upon evil in all of its entrenched power and persecuting force.

The fifth seal is not in chronological succession to the first four, but rather is simply in the succession of the visions. The plea of the souls under the altar was answered in the white robes of victory given to each one of them and in the call that they should "rest a little longer, until the number of their fellow servants and their brethren should be complete, who were to be killed as they themselves had been." God's great redemptive purpose in history must be worked out even though more suffering is involved. They were not transferred from beneath the altar. They were given white robes of victory while they wait for the consummation of God's purposes. Their rest is probably a reference to the rest mentioned in 14:13, "Blessed are the dead who die in the Lord henceforth." "Blessed indeed," says the Spirit, "that they may rest from their labors, for their deeds follow them!"

The Sixth Seal (6:12-17)

The descriptions in this seal are drawn from a number of passages. They indicate that we are looking to the great day of God's judgment. "The great day of their wrath has come" (17), when the vindication called for in the fifth seal will take place. Five great events accompany this day in the universe, and every detail is also found in the description of judgment in the Old Testament (Isa. 13:13; Ps. 102:25,26): the earthquake (Ezek. 38:18ff; Joel 2:10; Hag. 2:6,7), the sun becoming black like sackcloth and the moon becoming blood (Joel 2:31; Isa. 50:3), the stars falling like green, unripe figs swept off the tree prematurely by a strong wind, the rolling up of the heavens like a scroll (Isa. 34:4), the moving of the hills and the islands of the sea (Jer. 4:24; Nahum 1:5). The whole universe is convulsed and the most enduring things falls into chaos. Along with these convulsions of the earth and heavens, seven classes of mankind are mentioned: the kings, the princes, the chief captains or the military leaders, the strong, the slaves, and the freemen. All the godless world from the highest to the lowest classes is seized with the same fear (Joel 2:1), hiding in caves and rocks of the mountains, and calling for the mountains and rocks to cover them up and to hide them from the face of God and from the wrath of the Lamb (Hos. 10:8). This is a graphic, dramatic picture of the terror of evil men at the end and the inescapable judgment of God and the Lamb. As throughout the New Testament, the Lamb is also the judge. Note the expression "the wrath of the Lamb," even though he was called a Lion. One scarcely thinks of a Lamb being wrathful, but this indicates the justice and the judgment of God upon evil. The concluding question in this paragraph is, "Who is able to stand?" (Joel 2:11). As in the Garden of Eden sinful man hid from God, so shall it be man's desire at the end. There is no place to hide, though the first instinct of sinful man is to run for cover and to seek the darkness rather than stand in the face of God (John 3:19).

Scholars differ regarding the description of judgment here whether it refers to judgment brought upon men while the world still stands or is a reference to the last day. Our view is that it is a view of the last day, looked at proleptically here and more fully later.

Conclusion

This lesson has presented us with the four horsemen, representing conquest, strife, famine, and death. In contrast, the sufferings of those who have been slain because of their faith call for the vindication of righteousness in a godless world and the concluding seal emphasizes the terror of godless men as they confront the presence of God and Christ. The four horsemen of Revelation have ridden many times through human history, and the people of God have suffered persecution many times. The assurance of this lesson is that the persecuted triumph and the godless are judged.

Discussion Questions

1. Discuss the various approaches that have been taken toward this part of the Book of Revelation.

82

2. What relationship may be seen between the first four seals and the materials in Zechariah 6:1-8?

3. How has the first horse and rider been interpreted? What evidence is presented here for not identifying this rider with the rider in 19:11ff?

4. What does the bright red horse represent?

5. What is the significance of the statement about bread and its price?

6. Why would the oil and wine not be hurt?

7. What types of death are described in the fourth seal?

8. What is the significance of the souls underneath the altar?

9. Read and ponder carefully the Old Testament references in our lesson.

10. What is the significance of men hiding in caves and rocks of the mountain and wanting to be covered up from the face of God?

Lesson 10

GOD'S CARE FOR HIS PEOPLE
(Revelation 7:1-8:5)

Introduction

Between the sixth and the seventh seal there are two visions that are given to answer the question, "What about the people of God during this time? Are they to be forgotten? Or will God take care of them?" The first vision concerns the sealing of the 144,000, while the second vision describes the innumerable company around the throne in glory. The first vision concerns God's people upon earth, while the second looks to the ultimate consummation of God's great protection in the final salvation of his own. Despite the riding of the four horsemen, and the persecution of God's people, in the sealing of the 144,000 God's purpose is to bring them safely through any evil which the world with all of its power can bring upon them. This does not mean to say that God's people will be exempt from all tragedy and suffering. Rather, they shall be secured by an inner spiritual sealing so that passing through the fires of suffering they shall not be hurt.

Those who hold to the futurist view interpret this to refer to the Jewish Christians that are sealed after the coming of Christ and the "rapture" of the saints in the sky. The nation of Israel has been converted and these are now sealed. But this overlooks the fact that the expression "servants of our God" (vs. 3) refers to the same group addressed in chapter one in the introduction (1:1). Throughout the New Testament fleshly

Israel is a type of spiritual Israel, the church, God's people under the New Covenant. The church is the true Israel of God today (Rom. 2:28,29; Gal. 3:29; 6:16; Phil. 3:3; James 1:1; 1 Pet. 1:1; 2:9,10). In addition, previous references in the Book of Revelation indicate that John regards Christians as the true Jews (Rev. 2:9; 3:9). Also in chapter 14:1 this same group is pictured on Mount Zion sharing the triumph of the Lamb. Thus the 144,000 described in terms of the twelve tribes on earth refer to God's true spiritual Israel on earth, being protected by his seal and brought safely through the tribulations. This same group of people is spoken of as the great multitude which no man could number out of every tribe, tongue, people, and nation, standing about the throne of God and of the Lamb in heaven in the second vision. If this interpretation is correct, the sealing is an act by God embracing all his people, both Jews and Gentiles and continues in every generation until the end of this age. God assures the faithful that they will come safely through under his protection and he promises them for their encouragement the ultimate triumph of everlasting peace and joy.

Sealing of the 144,000 (7:1-6)

John's first view shows four angels standing at the four corners of the earth at all the four points of the compass, holding the four winds that blow from north, east, south, and west. They keep in check these winds so that no wind may hurt the earth and sea until the sealing is finished. Nothing is to prevent God from protecting his own. "The seal of the living God" is to be placed upon the foreheads of his servants. This book does not satisfy any further our curiosity as to what happens when the four angels turn loose the four winds to blow upon the earth and sea, but the imagination can lead us to understand that perhaps these represent in various ways the judgments that are to come as a storm upon the earth. Possibly these may refer to the judgments that are represented in the trumpets by way of warning to the earthdwellers. One of the important lessons of this book is that God makes use of the evil in the world in order to bring judgment upon evildoers.

Evil bears in itself the seeds of its own destruction. God makes use of the tragedies that men cause in order to bring about the destruction of evil men. The winds the four angels control are winds of woe (7:2). Another angel, used as God's agent for sealing the children of God, commands that these four angels shall not turn loose their winds of woe until the work of sealing has been consummated.

"The seal of the living God" refers to a common use in the ancient world of the seal in everyday life. The tomb of Jesus was sealed by the Roman governor Pilate to protect it from tampering (Matt. 27:66). The seal also denoted ownership (2 Tim. 2:19), "the Lord knows those who are his." The expression "the living God" is a familiar expression in the New Testament and emphasizes the difference between the God who not only lives forever but also is the source of life everlasting and the dead gods of the pagan world.

Note that this seal is placed upon the forehead and will be later referred to in contrast to the "mark of the beast" which is the distinguishing mark of those who follow this agent of the dragon (13:16,17).

John does not actually see the sealing; he only hears the number of the sealed. This number, 144,000, is a symbolic number, since the same number comes from each one of twelve tribes and each tribe is named one by one. This is intended to signify the fullness or full number of God's people. Those who would limit it to the elect from Israel in the Old Testament have missed the Christian emphasis of this book. Those who would limit it to only the Jewish Christians have missed the significance of the church being the true Israel of God today.

The listing of the tribes would certainly not refer to Israel in the flesh, for a number of the tribes had already lost their identity by New Testament times. In fact, many Jews could not trace their tribal connection. The order in which the tribes are listed is strange, but when one reads the Old Testament he will find at least 19 different arrangements in the listing of the tribes there. Judah heads this list where he would expect Reuben. Probably Judah's heading the list is intended to focus attention upon this tribe as the one from which the Messiah came. In the list Dan is omitted, and Joseph is substituted for the name Ephraim. Ephraim and Manasseh were sons of Joseph. Irenaeus (about A.D. 185) explained the omission of Dan as due to the belief that the antichrist would come from the tribe of Dan (*Against Heresies*, v. 30.2). This may be the reason why Dan is omitted here, although it is simply a conjecture.

Innumerable Company (7:9-17)

In this second vision John sees the whole multitude of the redeemed, now a company "which no man could number," coming from all over the world and standing before the throne of the Lamb. They are now clothed with the white robes of their victory and palm branches are in their hands, as they join in a great cry of triumph. The theme of their cry is "salvation," for they have been redeemed eternally and ascribe their redemption to God and to the Lamb. Here the One who sits upon the throne is described as "our God," thus interpreting this particular statement definitely, if there were any doubt about its meaning previously. The true Savior is not the emperor who loved the title *Soter*, meaning Savior, but the true Savior is Jesus Christ and our God. Joining the circle of worshippers around the throne is the great company of angels, and they fall upon their faces and offer their own hymn of praise. It is a sevenfold ascription of praise to God beginning with the *Amen*, by which they sanction the cry of the redeemed. The definite article is used in the Greek with each one of these seven elements in this doxology, but the order in which these come is different from other doxologies found in the book. These glories are ascribed to God for all eternity.

One of the elders asks a question of John, not for the purpose of gaining information, but for purposes of identifying the scene, and particularly the ones that are in the scene and from where they had come. John's answer indicates he would like to know the answer to that question. The elder then identifies the ones wearing the white robes as those who had been sinners, for they had washed their robes and made them white in the blood of the Lamb. Their sins had been forgiven through their response to Jesus Christ. One of the figures in the Scriptures describing sin looks upon it as that which makes the spirit of an individual dirty, and redemption is described in terms of cleansing from the uncleanness and defilement of sin. These are also the ones who have come through the great tribulation, the time of persecution and great suffering, and have been faithful and true. They had realized the promises to the ones that conquer specifically made in the letters to the seven churches. Thus they are always before the throne of God, serving him in his temple and his protection is upon them. The word translated "shall spread his tabernacle" (ASV) (Gr. *skenoo*) is defined in the Arndt-Gingrich Lexicon as "live" or "dwell," but specifically in this passage as "shelter." God's presence is with his people and his protection shields them forever. As his seal had protected them on earth, they are now made secure through all eternity.

Drawing upon language found in Isaiah 49:10, the protection is further described. They shall know hunger and thirst no more, nor suffer because of the blazing heat. Their days of privation and hardship are finished. Their "slight momentary affliction" (2 Cor. 4:17) is contrasted to eternity around God's throne. The next verse (17) presents us with the Lamb as the shepherd of his people. While the KJV translates this word "feed," the Greek word literally means "act as a shepherd" and is so translated in ASV, RSV. (See similarly Acts 20:28.) This is a favorite figure in the writings of John. Interestingly, the Lamb as their shepherd has taken on their nature as sheep. We do not think of a lamb being the shepherd of a flock, but this Lamb who took on the nature of his sheep now is their shepherd. He is the Good Shepherd who laid down his life for his sheep (John 10:11). As he has guided them through life in this world, this passage shows that his shepherding will continue to "guide them to springs of living water, and God will wipe away every tear from their eyes." Like a mother wiping away tears from the eyes of little children, so God wipes away our tears. This language is drawn from Isaiah (25:8) and must have been of particular comfort to those early Christians as they have to later generations of the faithful.

There are several parallels in this section to the last two chapters of the Bible. Here the description of the new Jerusalem and the blessing of God's people are anticipated proleptically. Baljon stated about these verses, "Words like these of verses 15-17 sound like a divine music in the ears of the persecuted. God will comfort as a mother comforts."

The Seventh Seal (8:1-5)

With the opening of the seventh seal, the sealed book is now open and an expectant silence occurs in heaven. This dramatic silence ushers in the seven angels with the seven trumpets. Actually the entire group of seven trumpets composes the contents of the seventh seal. Praises of the angel hosts along with the elders and the four living creatures are stopped in order that the prayers of those saints (Christians) on earth may be heard.

The seven angels "who stand before God" were thought of as occupying a particular position by the Jews. The expression "to stand before" means to attend upon or to be the servant of someone. Gabriel describes himself as one who stands in the presence of God (Luke 1:19). In the Book of Tobit in the Jewish Apocrypha, we read, "I am Raphael, one of the seven holy angels which present prayers of the saints, and go in before the glory of the holy one" (12:15). From 1 Enoch, another apocryphal book, the names of the archangels are given as Gabriel, Raphael, Michael, Uriel, Raquel, Sariel, and Remiel. Only Gabriel and Michael appear in the New Testament. Whether the seven angels here mentioned in Revelation are archangels cannot be clearly determined.

The trumpet had a particular significance in the Old Testament. It was used not only in connection with warning, but also with the time of judgment (Joel 2:1ff). It is a sign of God's

89

intervention in this world's affairs (Ex. 19:16,19). In fact, we read in the New Testament of "the last trumpet" which shall accompany the coming of the Lord again (Matt. 24:31; 1 Cor. 15:52; 1 Thess. 4:16). These seven trumpets are trumpets of warning and judgment.

Next we see another angel who comes and stands at the altar with his golden censer and much incense is given to him "to mingle with the prayers of all the saints" that go up before God out of the angel's hand. The word "altar" is mentioned seven times in the Book of Revelation (6:9; 8:3 twice, 5; 9:13; 14:18; 16:7). The golden altar was the altar in the tabernacle that stood just before the veil which separated the Holy Place from the Holy of Holies. Here both morning and evening incense were offered to God from the golden censer filled with coals of fire from the brazen altar in the court and with incense from the table of the shewbread inside the tabernacle. The golden altar is here described as standing before the throne of God in heaven. Probably "much incense" represents Christ's intercession added to the saints' prayers, for he is the saints' Advocate with the Father (1 John 2:1). There is no idea here of a special angelic mediation in addition to Christ's, since throughout the book angels refuse to receive the worship of the prophet. Note again that "all the saints," the struggling, suffering saints on earth, are included. The prayers of the saints accompanied by the sweet perfume of the incense, representing Christ's intercession, are purged of everything selfish and come up acceptably before God. The answer to those prayers came in verse 5 when the censer was filled with fire from the altar and cast upon the earth. It is doubtful that two distinct altars appear in this passage, but probably characteristics of both the golden altar and the altar of burnt offering are combined in this altar. Obviously, no sacrifices of blood would be offered upon the altar of burnt offering in heaven, since one full and complete sacrifice had already been given. It is better to understand the altar as partaking of the nature of both these Old Testament counterparts. The "thunders, voices, flashes of lightning, and an earthquake" are also associated with the seventh trumpet (11:19) and the seventh bowl (16:18). The judgments of God upon a wicked world are about to be given.

We have now studied the seven seals. The next lesson will present the seven trumpets, and Book II, Lesson 4 will present the seven bowls. Striking parallels exist between these three sections of the book. The beginning of the eighth chapter sets the stage for the events connected with the trumpets.

Discussion Questions

1. What questions are the two visions of chapter seven designed to answer for the reader?

2. What evidence do we have for saying that the church is spiritual Israel today?

3. What interpretations have been given to the 144,000 by various commentators? What meaning would you give to this?

4. What meanings are attached in the Bible to sealing? What assurances does God give his people in sealing them?

5. What explanations have been given regarding the listing of the tribes here and the omission?

6. Describe the scene in the second part of this vision around the throne of God. Who are the ones in white garments and how were their garments made white?

7. What is the meaning of the expression "shall spread his tabernacle over them"?

8. Can you draw some parallels between this passage and the last two chapters of this book?

9. What connection does the seventh seal have with the seven trumpets?

10. What significance does the trumpet have in both the Old and the New Testaments? How are we to understand it here?

11. What meaning do you see in the incense offered to God and the "much incense" added to that which is offered before him? Are there other Scriptures that might shed some light upon this? If so, what are they?

12. What three sections of Revelation show striking parallels?

Lesson 11

THE SIX TRUMPETS
(Revelation 8:6-9:21)

Introduction

The seven trumpets like the seven seals divide themselves conveniently into two groups, the first four similar to the plagues of Egypt, and last three of a more terrible and unique aspect. Apparently from the partial nature of the judgments, these do not represent the last of God's judgments, but they anticipate that last one.

Like Egypt of old, the world today is in opposition to God and can be described as afflicting and holding in bondage the people of God. These warnings come to make men realize that God is sovereign ruler of the universe and wicked men need to seek his will.

The First Trumpet (8:7)

At the sounding of the first trumpet, hail and fire mingled with blood are cast upon the earth and the vegetation is affected. The earth with all of its plant life and trees experiences a third part destroyed and all green grass lost. Just as in Zechariah 13:8,9, the fraction expresses a partial but not the final destruction. One is reminded here of the seventh plague of hail and fire in Exodus 9:24. The partial destruction gives men an opportunity for repentance and turning to God.

93

The Second Trumpet (8:8,9)

At the sounding of the second trumpet, "something like a great mountain, burning with fire" was cast into the sea. A mountain ablaze (or being moved) in the Old Testament symbolized great trouble and commotion (Ps. 46:2; Isa. 54:10; Ezek. 38:20; Mic. 1:4; Nahum 1:5). "A third of the sea became blood, a third of the living creatures in the sea died, and a third of the ships were destroyed." Like the Nile smitten in the first plague, the sea became blood (Ex. 7:20,21). As the first trumpet had affected the vegetation and plant life of the earth, the second trumpet affects the sea and its life. Not even in the vast sea can man escape God's warning judgments, yet God does not here completely destroy.

The Third Trumpet (8:10,11)

The sounding of the third trumpet affects the fresh water supply. A flaming meteor "blazing like a torch" fell from heaven upon the fresh waters and springs. The symbolic name of the flaming star is Wormwood. Wormwood water is more than once used in the Old Testament as a symbol of suffering for evil-doing (Jer. 9:15; 23:15). Wormwood mixed with water does not kill, but "a third of the waters became wormwood," and men died because of this change. This is the reverse of the miracle at Marah, where the bitter waters were made sweet (Ex. 15:23-25). Wormwood is also used as a metaphor for injustice and unrighteousness (Amos 5:7; 6:12) and is a synonym for poisonous water as a metaphor of God's punishments (Jer. 9:15; 23:15). Even the waters became contaminated and bitter.

The Fourth Trumpet (8:12)

The sounding of the fourth angel brings on darkness on a third of the sun, moon, and stars and resembles the ninth plague of darkness in Egypt (Ex. 10:21ff). This is a visitation upon the heavenly bodies following the judgments upon the earth and its plant life, the sea and its creatures and life, and the fresh waters. These also have a profound effect on men as well. It would appear that the force of these four trumpets is to show that the entire universe is used by God to warn and to call men to repentance. In fact, this would appear to be the purpose of all of these trumpets. Also in resembling the exodus of the Old Testament, it is preparatory to God's final deliverance of his people.

The Eagle in Mid-Heaven (8:13)

The vision in verse 13 divides the first four trumpets from the last trumpets by introducing the three woes. John sees and hears the eagle, the strongest of birds, flying through mid-heaven crying, "Woe, woe, woe to those who dwell on the earth" (the rebellious world). This expression "those who dwell on the earth" is used throughout this book to denote the earth-bound, unbelieving, rebellious, sinful, this-worldly inhabitants of the earth. These woes come because of the nature of the tumpets blown by the three angels, yet to sound. This reminds us that the woes are negative side of the gospel's blessings, as Jesus showed in Luke 6:24-26. God intends to arouse men to see their terrible condition apart from him and to place the responsibility for the evil and tragedy of the world upon the wickedness of men.

The Fifth Trumpet (9:1-12)

The fifth trumpet brings the plague of demonic locusts from the bottomless pit or the underworld. As God has used the forces and powers of nature to warn men, he now makes use of the demonic forces of evil from the "bottomless pit" for the ultimate righteous purposes he has in the world. The vision here represents probably an angel, "a star," to whom is given "the key to the shaft of the bottomless pit." The meaning may be no more than that John saw an angel coming down from heaven to open this pit. Several interpretations of the pit have been given. Some equate it with Tartarus mentioned as the intermediate abode of fallen spirits (2 Pet. 2:4). Others think of it as the final place of punishment for the fallen angels and demons, a burning furnace, the smoke of which ascends upward forever. Others think of it as the final place of punishment for Satan, the demons, and wicked men. Probably the first view seems the more likely in view of Luke 8:31. Rev. 20:1,3 says it was into this bottomless pit that Satan, after he was bound, was cast.

The pit is seen here as closed and locked, but the star with the key opens the pit and at its opening smoke like that from a great furnace rises up to darken the light of the sun and fill the air. Out of this smoke come the locusts that torment. The plague of locusts was the eighth of the Egyptian plagues (Ex. 10:1-20). Locusts were a particular scourge in that part of the world, invading cultivated areas and eating all vegetation. They bred in the desert, but traveled in huge hordes that looked like clouds on the horizon, and consumed every bit of available vegetation.

These are unusual locusts, however, for they do not hurt any grass "or any green growth or any tree." They only hurt men. In fact, the only men they can hurt are those that do not have "the seal of God upon their foreheads." They have power to torment those who live in the world, those who are opposed to God. They cannot torture those who have been sealed by God. Verse 4 of this chapter explains the significance of the sealing mentioned in 7:4-8. Like scorpions, the power of the locusts to torment is in their tails, for although a scorpion sting is extremely painful, it is not necessarily fatal. Some commentators see a contradiction between 9:4 and 8:7, but when the expression "all green grass" in 8:7 is understood to include that which is found in the third part of the world, there is no contradiction here. Only that part of the earth that is affected by the hail and fire mingled with blood will lose its grass.

The demonic locusts graphically picture the torment to the human spirit and human personality that evil brings. The smoke that rises to darken the sky brings with it the torments that make men cry out to die and desire death, yet find no death. This graphically expresses the slavery sin exerts over men. Repeatedly when men have followed their lusts, their greed and desire for glory, and have abandoned God and his way, they have experienced these same torments, like the torment of a scorpion. The five months they shall torment may be explained as the life span of a locust from birth to death. It certainly indicates that there is a limit to this torment, although exactly what this signifies is not clear. The prophet foresees the actions of those who are tormented as they suffer and want to die but are not able. Death habitually flees from them. This is the agony of a conscience that is stricken and of a life suffering under the torment of evil. Yet even the torture occurs in order that men may be brought to see the true nature of evil and turn from it in repentance. The nature of evil is to destroy, so that men following evil come to their own destruction.

The first six verses have described the origin and tormenting power of these locusts, but the seventh verse introduces us to a description drawn largely from Joel 2:2-11. This interesting passage describes their approach (2:2), their destruction of vegetation (2:3), their comparison to horses (2:4), their noise (2:5), their effect upon people (2:6), their marching array (2:7), their courage (2:8,9), their use as God's army (2:10,11). It would be good to read Joel 2:1-11 as background for this section.

In describing the locusts, John says they are like horses prepared for war. It is remarkable that the locust's head strikingly resembles a horse, so that in German the name for locust is derived from the word for horse. These locusts are wearing on their heads something that resembles crowns, like kings of torment and torture. Their faces resemble men's faces, their hair is like the hair of women, and their teeth like those of lions. Their breastplates are like breastplates of iron, and their wings like the sound of rushing chariots. The noise of the great masses of horsemen and chariots rushing to battle would be overwhelming. The stings in their tails, like scorpion stings, can hurt. Their king is called "the angel of the bottomless pit" and he is here given two names: in the Hebrew language, Abaddon, and in Greek, Apollyon, both meaning "Destroyer."

Verse 12 simply indicates that the first woe is past; two others are yet to come.

The Sixth Trumpet (9:13-21)

Following the demonic locusts, the sixth trumpet ushers in the most dreadful of all the woes, the great army of hellish horsemen. The voice from the four horns of the golden altar where the incense was offered to God commands the sixth angel after his blast to turn loose the four angels bound at the river Euphrates. They go forth to kill men, and one-third of mankind is slain. This may reflect the widespread fear that prevailed in the first century before Christ and in later years, that the major enemy of the Roman Empire were the Parthian horsemen and armies beyond the Euphrates. But would early Christians be praying to God for him to release the Parthian hordes on Rome? This is hard to believe. Barnes finds the fulfillment of this in the Turkish conquest of the Byzantine Empire with the fall of Constantinople, 1453. Yet really no actual invasion can quite parallel this symbolic invasion. While these interpretations may be appealing, it seems better to take this as we have taken other trumpets a symbolic of evil secular power that does its best to overcome and destroy God's power over men's lives.

The largest number in the book occurs here, "twice 10,000 times 10,000." John then describes these horses and horsemen. The horsemen had breastplates resembling glowing fire and sulphur with blue hyacinth playing the fiery sulphur. Turning to the description of the horses, from their mouths fire, smoke, and sulphur corresponding to the breastplates of the riders, proceed, and their heads are like heads of lions. The three plagues that killed the third part of men come from their mouths. But there is an additional power shared with their tails, for their tails resemble serpents and have heads to torment and wound, both heads and tails destroy and kill. Fire and sulphur are often associated with the punishment of evil, and the hellish nature of these horses and riders is indicated by the fire and sulphur associated with them as they kill. This is a warning made with the hope that man can see the self-defeating power of evil and turn to God in repentance. To men who will not respond to his word, God speaks through the evil they have brought upon themselves to learn from their tragic experiences and turn to him. Yet how often men repeat the same old mistakes and fail to learn from their moral failures and tragic experiences. They shut their eyes, close up their ears and refuse to heed the warnings.

The rest of the men who survived did not repent. They did not turn from their idolatrous worship which the New Testament considers the worship of demons (1 Cor. 10:20). They continued to bow down before their idols of gold, silver, bronze, stone, and wood, that could not respond or bless them. They refused to acknowledge the true Creator of gold, silver, bronze, stone and wood. They continued to walk in their ways of immorality and lustfulness. Their refusal to repent in spite of all the warnings given shows the hardened character of their sinful hearts. Yet these warnings show the mercy of God, and vindicate his justice in leaving men without excuse as they reject his revelation, spurn his salvation, and close up their lives to his warnings.

Conclusion

As the first four trumpets have brought God's warning trumpet call in natural calamities of land, sea, fresh waters, and heavens, the fifth trumpet has brought the torment of demonic locusts that take peace and happiness away from man's spirit. The sixth trumpet has presented God's judgment in the warfare and terrific devilish horsemen, killing and slaughtering men as if to say that these are man's own God-defying efforts turned against him. What a startling, terrifying picture to a sinful, rebellious world!

Discussion Questions

1. What similarities to and difference from the plagues of Egypt do you see in the trumpets as described here?

2. What significance may be attached to the fractions used in the trumpet scenes?

3. What significance do you see in the eagle flying in mid-heaven?

4. What interpretations have been given to the bottomless pit mentioned in the fifth trumpet? How do you understand it?

5. In what ways were locusts a scourge to the Near East?

6. What meanings do you see in these demonic locusts? Can you think of various ways in which sin causes pain and suffering to human beings?

7. What description is given here of the demonic locusts? Compare the passage in Joel with the one here and note the similarity.

8. What interpretations are given to the army of hellish horsemen in the sixth trumpet?

9. What three plagues come from the mouths of the horses?

10. What do the trumpets show about God and what effect do they have on the world at large? What significance do you see in the trumpets in this lesson?

Lesson 12

CERTAINTY OF THE END
(Revelation 10:1-11)

Introduction

As John saw the visions of chapter 7 between the opening of the sixth and seventh seals, so the visions of chapter 10 and the first part of chapter 11 occur between the sixth and seventh trumpets. In the tenth chapter the certainty of the end is affirmed. John is further commissioned as a prophet to continue his work of prophesying, particularly assuring the church during the time of the warning judgments. God never leaves very far away the question of the care of his church in this book. The materials in this lesson are not so difficult to understand as in some of the other lessons that we have studied. The Book of Revelation is a book with very difficult passages, and when we come to study one of these we have to take more than usual space in order to see how it has been interpreted and evaluate these interpretations. We are not confronted in chapter 10 with so many puzzles as we shall be in the following chapter.

The Strong Angel (10:1-7)

This scene opens with the prophet once more transferred back to earth, although he does not mention the change in the text. He saw "another mighty angel coming down from heaven" similar to the one in 5:2 who uttered the call throughout the universe to find the one worthy to open the seals of the closed book. The mighty angel here was clothed in a cloud and had a rainbow over his head. The rainbow is connected with the glory that surrounds the throne of God (4:3). His face shone like the sun, and his legs were flaming like pillars of fire. Some have interpreted this angel to be Christ himself, but against this interpretation is the fact that Christ is nowhere else in all the New Testament spoken of as an angel. Angels are created beings of a spiritual rank, while Christ as the Son of God shares the full nature of the Godhead and is eternal. Surely he could not be called *"another mighty angel."* However, the description given concerning this angel indicates that he is closely associated with the presence of God and Christ, and therefore the announcement he has to make is of tremendous significance.

In his hand is a little book that is opened, in contrast to the sealed book in chapter 5. This is not a closed book; this is an open book, which indicates that it will show a part of God's great purposes. Because it is a little book it indicates that it will contain not all of the divine purposes for the universe, but only a part of those purposes. To understand the contents of it in particular, one must await until verse eleven. Planting his right foot on the sea and his left on the earth, he stands astride the world and his great voice like the roaring of a lion cries out to all the universe (Joel 3:16). The lion's roar is used as a symbol of God's message in the Old Testament (Amos 3:8). Because the angel has come down as a mighty one from heaven and speaks in this great shout, we are reminded once more that this is a revelation from God. Accompanying his shout, the seven thunders are heard, but their message is not revealed. What the seven thunders said is kept from us at the command of heaven, and there is no need to try to speculate about the nature of the seven thunders. John records the fact that he was ready to write down what was uttered by the seven thunders when the command came to seal up the things that the seven thunders had uttered and not write them down. In this case the sealing is the equivalent of not writing. No doubt this is an allusion to Daniel 12:4,9 where the prophet is commanded to keep his visions secret until the end. Daniel is commanded to seal up the words of his prophecy. Sometimes a revelation is given that is not possible to pass on to men. This apparently is what the apostle Paul conveys to us in 2 Corinthians 12:4, when he describes a man, probably himself, who heard words that it was not lawful for a man to utter. He did not reveal these words. Perhaps the revelation might be more than a generation of men could accept, but at any rate what the seven thunders uttered was not passed on.

Now the prophet sees the angel lift his right hand in a great oath to swear by God who lives forever and ever and who has created the heavens, the earth, the sea, and all that exists within them "that there should be no more delay." The raised hand toward heaven is the customary gesture for taking an oath before the God who dwells in heaven (Dan. 12:7; Deut. 32:40). Two understandings of this passage are reflected in the translations given in English. The one quoted above taken from the RSV emphasizes that there will be no more delay in carrying out and fulfilling God's own promise to complete his purpose and to bring his kingdom to its consummation. The KJV, however, translates this part of the verse "that there should be time no longer." This means that the time has come for the end. Whichever rendering is followed, there is not a great difference in the actual meaning, since such a declaration as this is followed by the giving of the book to the prophet and his command to continue prophesying. The whole scene is intended to affirm the fact that God will complete his purpose. The promise is that in the days of the voice of the seventh angel when he is about to sound, "the mystery of God" will be finished. The word "mystery" in the New Testament is often used concerning the purpose of God to indicate that which has been hidden or only partially revealed but is now to be made fully manifest. It does not carry with it the significance of the mysterious. The mystery here is connected with the good tidings that God has declared to his servants, the prophets. The prophets referred to are the prophets under the New Testament, and the revelation of God's final purpose is to be in accordance with the gospel that he has revealed to his inspired prophets. The term "mystery" is used because the world does not really know what God is working out through the ages for the redemption of mankind, and the world cannot know this purpose except by the revelation which God supplies. Because God has declared his revelation to his prophets, and they have conveyed this to the church, the church can walk in the hope and light of the revelation of God's will. God is faithful and can be relied upon by Christians to carry out that which he has purposed and promised. This can be a great consolation to Christians, particularly in times of persecution and distress such as these early Christians were undergoing.

The Little Book and the Prophet (10:8-11)

The same voice that had forbidden him from heaven to write down the voices of the seven thunders in verse four now gives the command to John to go up to the angel and take the book that is open upon his hand. The verb translated "go" really has the force of intensifying the command, just as we often say, "Go do this," or "Go do that." Obviously this is a symbolic action, since John would surely be dwarfed in size before the enormous figure of the angel astride both land and sea. However, this is not to be considered, since we have here symbolism indicating how this word from God comes to the prophet.

John did as he was commanded to do, asking that the angel give him the little book. The angel commanded him to take the book and eat it up. Literally, the Greek word used here means to "eat it down," indicating that it will go down into his stomach. Our idiom is different. We say, "Eat it up." By this is meant that he is to take it and fully understand it, spiritually to masticate it. Some commentators see in this statement the significance that God never forces his revelation upon anyone, but that his messenger must be a willing one to take that which is put before him.

John is told that in eating it he will find it will be sweet in his mouth like honey but bitter in his stomach. This has been called "bittersweet." There is a mixture of sweet and bitter in what he will say. God's promises and God's judgment make up the bittersweet. The idea of sweetness connected with God's word occurs in the Scriptures (Ps. 19:10; 119:103). The command to eat this book seems a strange one, but it recalls the experience of Ezekiel the prophet in the Old Testament (Ezek. 2:9—3:3). Many commentators interpret the little book open upon the angel's hand now taken by John, to contain everything in the Book of Revelation after the sounding of the seventh trumpet. In other words, the last part of the book is connected with the little book opened. This one deals with the church and its great foes and struggles, rather than with the full range of God's purposes for the whole universe. Other commentators would more especially relate this to the materials in the 11th chapter. At any rate, it would appear that what is involved for John is to continue to prophesy concerning God's will about peoples, nations, tongues, and kings. This indicates that the former view is the more correct one, that the message of the latter part of the book is involved here. What this amounts to is simply a recommissioning of John to do his great work of prophesying.

John records his experience in taking the book and eating it. He finds that what the angel has told him becomes true for him. The two aspects of the prophet's activities are emphasized—the bitter and the sweet. These two aspects of any proclamation of God's word come clearly to the fore. No one can proclaim God's word without emphasizing the mercy and love, the gracious provisions of God's redemption for man. But the bitter part has to do with the judgments and the warnings regarding evil, sin, and rebellion to the will of God. No one can be true to the divine relation who does not combine the bitter and the sweet. This is not to say that God's people delight in the judgments and the warnings, but rather recognize that there are these two aspects in the revelation of God's will.

In this lesson we are once more reminded of God's sovereign lordship over history and the commission given to the prophet is that of continuing to show how his divine purposes will be worked out to the victory of his people and his righteousness.

Discussion Questions

1. Describe the mighty angel. How does this description show us his close connection with the throne of God and of the Lamb?

2. Why is it questionable to interpret the mighty angel as referring to Christ?

3. What significance attaches to the opened book?

4. What meaning do you see in the command given to John not to record the voices of the seven thunders?

5. Can you think of other instances of swearing a solemn oath in the Bible?

6. How would you reconcile the taking of this solemn oath with Jesus' teaching on oaths in Matthew 5:34-37?

7. What two views are represented in the translations concerning the meaning of verse seven? Evaluate these.

8. What is the meaning of "mystery" in this passage?

9. What other instance in the Bible do we have of a prophet "eating a book"? What is the meaning of the command to eat this book?

10. Describe John's experience in eating the book.

11. How are we to understand the bitter and the sweet in the prophet's words?

Lesson 13

PROTECTION OF GOD'S PEOPLE DURING TRIBULATION
(Revelation 11:1-19)

Introduction

Perhaps no part of the Book of Revelation has given more difficulty to interpreters than the eleventh chapter. Many things about it continue to puzzle the student, and many points remain obscure. Some of the conclusions expressed in this lesson are tentative and are given in the full recognition that one cannot be dogmatic about a passage as difficult as this one. The position one takes on this passage is usually controlled by the major approach he has taken to other sections of the book. For that reason our interpretations will be guided by the general positions we have taken in approaching the teachings of this book.

Major Approaches

It is helpful for the student prior to studying this passage to be aware of the major approaches taken by scholars to such a controversial chapter. Three major approaches interpret the passage literally. There are those who see this chapter fulfilled in the fall of Jerusalem in A.D. 70. The conflict is one between unbelieving Israel and Jewish Christians. The temple's inner part refers to God's people protected by God, while the court without refers to unbelieving Israel. Forty-two months and equivalent time periods refer to the period of the Jewish War particularly under Vespasian's leadership. The two witnesses refer to Jewish Christian preachers prophesying during the War, who are later killed by the Romans. Jerusalem falls, and then Christianity is liberated from Judaism and can spread worldwide. This obviously depends on dating the book during the reign of Nero, and finds its major message to Jewish Christians undergoing the privations of the fall of Jerusalem.

The second approach is an extreme preterist approach also in that it views the chapter as a reference to the Jewish War (A.D. 66-70). This view is that the passage is based on a Zealot prophecy written before the fall of Jerusalem which said that the temple would not be taken in the war. It would be preserved by God from destruction, and those who were within would be saved. Of course this did not occur historically, for the Romans destroyed the temple along with the city. The chapter is composed of various elements put together without much thought of unity. This view does not have a place for divine inspiration. If we believe that the book is what it claims to be, a divinely inspired prophecy, we can dismiss this particular approach.

The third approach is the futurist view also known as dispensational premillennialism held by those strongly believing in the inspiration of this book. The futurist view does not apply the passage to the church, but separates the church and Israel as two separate entities. It looks for a literal restoration of the Jews to Palestine fulfilling all the prophecies of the Old Testament concerning a return from exile. It does not apply those prophecies to the return after the Babylonian captivity. It literally interprets the forty-two months as the three and one-half years during which the city of Jerusalem will be trampled down and defiled by unbelieving Gentiles. The beast is the revived Roman Empire making war against the Jewish saints, slaying the two witnesses who are finally vindicated at the first resurrection. This makes the book essentially a Jewish book, not a Christian one centered in the church as God's people today. As we have pointed out previously, it separates the book from the people to whom it was originally addressed. For this and other reasons we do not follow this view.

The continuous historical approach applies this chapter to the Roman Catholic Church, measured by the standard of God's word. The line between the true and the false church was drawn at the Reformation. The two witnesses symbolize those who protest against Roman Catholicism with the war of the beast representing Roman Catholic persecution. The triumphal resurrection of the two witnesses is the breaking forth of the Reformation and the acceptance of the Reformation's doctrine. We have given reasons earlier why we do not subscribe to this point of view.

The preterist approach refers this to the people of Israel in general with the inner court being the Christian court, and the outer court those who do not accept Christ and are rejected. The two witnesses symbolize the preaching activity of the church during the time of the persecuting Roman Empire. The witnesses killed symbolize the martyrdom of the preachers, and their rising from the dead symbolize the victory of the Christian cause with the edict of toleration under Constantine the Great, the Roman emperor who first granted Christianity official recognition. This approach finds the fulfillment of this passage in the centuries immediately following the writing of the apostle and finds little or nothing connected with the present time in its message. Many things about this interpretation are appealing. But if one believes that the church drifted away from the scriptures and the purity of New Testament Christianity this interpretation causes problems. If this chapter pictures the triumph of the church over the persecution of the Roman empire and the union of church and state under Constantine in the fourth century, this means that God has placed his stamp of divine approval on the church-state type of union which that period produced. Since this writer does not believe that the New Testament teaches such a union of church and state with its accompanying features, he finds it hard to see the Book of Revelation placing God's approval on this arrangement. If one, however, interprets the symbols here to promise triumph for Christians who faithfully endure persecutions not only in the time of the Roman empire, but in other times of tribulation, he does not have to ally this chapter with any Constantinian arrangement. The church will be what it was in New Testament days, made up of believers who had voluntarily obeyed the gospel of Christ.

This writer believes that the eleventh chapter describes God's protection of his people and their security in the midst of persecutions and tribulations not only in the early centuries but through the ages, particularly during the times when the beast, as an agent of the dragon, will persecute God's people. The two witnesses like Moses and Elijah proclaim God's word, and meet opposition and persecution and death and this is not limited to the early centuries or to any one particular period within the Christian age. Now let us turn to an examination of the passage itself.

The Measured Sanctuary (11:1,2)

This section is not introduced as a vision with such expressions as "I beheld" or "after this I saw." Instead, John is given a measuring rod with which to "measure the temple of God" which is the inner sanctuary of the temple, with its altar and those who worship there. At this time (the end of the first century) the temple at Jerusalem had been destroyed. In that temple only the priests could come into the inner sanctuary. In view of the fact that in this book the true Jews are Christians, this would symbolize the church and the faithful. The court outside the temple and "the holy city," now trodden underfoot, represent those who are in the world. Some interpreters would refer these to the unfaithful Christians who had apostatized from the faith. It is clear that only those inside the sanctuary are the ones who receive the protection of the Lord. Just as the sealing of the 144,000 in chapter seven signifies his protection, so the measuring of the temple signifies his protection. Note the passages in which the church is described as a spiritual house, a temple (1 Cor. 3:16; 2 Cor. 6:16; Eph. 2:20,21; 1 Pet. 2:5). The measuring here is for the purpose of preservation and protection, since the outer court is given over to be trampled under by the spiritual Gentiles, those of the world. One is impressed here with the fact that God has not forgotten his people in the time of calamity and difficulty. The length of time during which "the holy city" is trodden underfoot by the Gentiles is forty-two months (11:2). The expressions "forty-two months" (11:2), "one thousand two hundred and sixty days" (11:3; 12:6), and "a time, and times, and half a time" (12:14), are all equivalent expressions for three and one-half years during which the church is described as being afflicted. Just what the precise significance of this is has caused great controversy. Some have interpreted this to symbolize a special time of persecution that will come upon the church, either at one specific period before the end, when a personal antichrist appears, or at periodic times of tribulation, which, though limited, still bring God's people under severe persecution. Others have interpreted this to symbolize the entire period from the beginning of the church on Pentecost to the second coming of Christ. This represents the Christian dispensation throughout as a time of persecution and opposition and a time during which anti-Christian forces will oppose God's people. This same length of time occurs in Daniel 7:25; 12:7. Some see in the three and one-half years, or the equivalent expressions, the half of a complete seven, which is a perfect number, and therefore a symbol purely of the inadequate efforts to overcome the people of God.

The Two Witnesses (11:3-14)

The two witnesses that shall prophesy one thousand two hundred and sixty days are "clothed in sackcloth," indicative of the emphasis in their witnessing or proclamation—repentance. Who are these two witnesses? In their behavior, they obviously bear relationships to both Moses as the great lawgiver and Elijah as the great prophet of the Old Testament. The following interpretations have been given of these two witnesses. (1) Some have said these referred to the law and the prophets of the Old Testament or to the Old and the New Testaments with their double witness. (2) Others have thought of these referring to two actual persons, like the two men from the Old Testament. (3) Still others have interpreted these representing the church in its total witness-bearing to the world through its preachers or ministers of the word. The idea of expressing this time in terms of days has suggested the thought that perhaps this witnessing was to be a day after day affair.

111

In verse four these are called "the two olive trees, and the two lampstands which stand before the Lord," a clear reference to the vision of Zechariah 4. In Zechariah on either side of the golden lampstand are two olive trees that feed the lampstand with their fatness. These two trees probably represent Joshua, the priest, and Zerubbabel, and the lampstand represents Israel. In our present vision the two witnesses are the two lampstands bearing the light of God's word and, like two olive trees full of fatness, they continue to express this witnessing of the gospel to the world. These two witnesses represent the church, full of God's Spirit, that gives light to the world. Like Jeremiah (Jer. 5:14), the judging word, the warning word that calls to repentance and life which they proclaim, is like a devouring fire that will destroy those that are their foes—the ones who oppose the word. This figure also reminds one of the consuming fire that came down at the call of Elijah and devoured his enemy (2 Kings 1:9,10). Like Elijah of old, the two witnesses have power to shut up the heaven, that it rain not during the time of their prophesying. Like Moses, the lawgiver, they have power over the waters, to turn them to blood and to bring plagues upon the earth. They do this "as often as they desire" not to indicate willful acts, but rather to indicate that their desires are the desires of God.

It would be hard to understand how these two witnesses could refer to two specific individuals, especially since the beast is described as making "war upon them"; but this could be readily applied to the church (13:7). The beast is here closely associated with the bottomless pit, and is a demonic force in league with Satan. The witnesses are killed by the beast and their bodies lie unburied in the street of the great city that is called figuratively ("allegorically" RSV) Sodom, because it symbolizes the wickedness of the ancient city, and Egypt, because it held God's people in bondage. This great city was where Christ was crucified! Scholars differ whether there is any direct reference to the literal city of Jerusalem or whether this is simply symbolically a reference to the worldly anti-Christian power. The unbelieving world rejoices over the martyred forms, apparently a reference to the church undergoing a time of tremendous persecution and hostility. "After the three and one-half days" (11), a short but clearly defined period, the breath of life from God enters again into them, and they are raised up to the great amazement of the world, having a new divine life from above. They are caught up to the very throne of God. It would appear that what this passage is saying is that Christians must not feel because Christ has overcome they will have no more suffering, defeat, and martyrdom. The very nature of the gospel is to bring the church into conflict with the world and the world makes war upon it. The world is in its unbelieving activity actively hostile to God when it feels the strongest; and thus the figure of the beast that comes up out of the bottomless pit, mentioned in verse seven, foreshadows descriptions of the beast in chapter thirteen, and shows the hostility toward God which a world dominated by rebellious principles will have. Again and again when the church in its preaching and witnessing power seems overwhelmed, it has been revived and caught up to glory. The great earthquake that causes a tenth part of the city to fall so that there are others that are frightened and give glory to God in heaven are thought by some scholars to refer to repentance, but by many others to refer to no repentance whatsoever. Perhaps no parallel is intended, but one is reminded of the fact that Christ was in the tomb three days and nights, and these lie unburied for three and one-half days. The wicked have been tormented by the proclamations of warnings and the calls to repentance, by the fearful miracles (5,6) and by causing the consciences of men to be pricked. What the number 7,000 signifies still puzzles a number of scholars. Some think it is simply an estimation of a tenth of the population of Jerusalem in the time when this book was written. Others feel that it is only a symbolic number as a part of the whole.

The cryptic announcement of verse fourteen is that the second woe is passed and a third woe, which is the last of the three, is about to come.

The Seventh Trumpet (11:15-19)

The difficulty of this section is that we have here what would

113

appear to be an announcement of the final victory and triumph of Christ, yet there is almost half of the book still to be explored. For this reason those who look at the book not as a consecutive chronological pattern, but see it exhibiting some elements of parallelism, that is, parallel sections looking toward the end and viewing different aspects with a view to that end, find here a basis for the fact that we are looking now at the consummation of it all.

When the seventh angel sounds great voices in heaven announce, "The kingdom of the world has become the kingdom of our Lord and of his Christ and he shall reign forever and ever." Note that the kingdom of our Lord and his Christ is the same kingdom. His reign is a reign that lasts forever and ever. The next statement of the twenty-four elders enlarges upon this previous announcement. They fall upon their faces and worship God and say their words of praise. "Thou hast taken thy great power and begun to reign." Their cry identifies the time of this seventh trumpet as the time "for the dead to be judged, for rewarding thy servants, the prophets and saints, and those who fear thy name, both small and great; and for destroying the destroyers of the earth." It would appear that this is a view of the last judgment. The nations in their wrath have rebelled to the limit against God; and God's wrath has come in judgment upon them. The time has come also to reward the faithful, to give to the prophets and the saints and those who have lived in reverence of God's name, both small and great, the reward that is promised to them in the gospel. Obviously this points to God's great sovereignty. He has overcome all. His judgment has been visited upon all rebellious mankind. The saints have been rewarded and the sinners destroyed.

Among some scholars verse nineteen is connected with chapter twelve, as a kind of prelude to the vision there. However, if one looks at it as it is divided according to our chapter division, he finds this is the closing scene, the consummation. In opening the sanctuary of God in heaven the ark of his covenant is seen, showing that the veil which separated the Holy and the Most Holy Places has been taken away and men are able to look in to the very presence of God. Yet the whole consummation must be more fully described and the incidents of that little book that was left open must be declared in their bitter sweetness. The remaining lessons in the second book will involve the message chapters twelve through twenty-two.

Discussion Questions

1. Describe the major elements of the two literal interpretations of this chapter.

2. What symbolic approaches have been taken to the materials in this chapter?

3. What do we know about the temple in Jerusalem that can parallel the material in the first part of this chapter?

4. What is the significance of the forty-two months?

5. What characters in the Old Testament are alluded to in the two witnesses, and what incidents of their lives are referred to in this passage of Scripture?

6. What prophetic vision in the Old Testament contains two olive trees and a lampstand as a part of its imagery?

7. What indignities do the unbelievers heap upon the dead bodies of the witnesses?

8. What significance might be drawn from the fact that the breath of life from God enters into them and they stand upon their feet?

9. What indications from the Scriptures given in connection with the seventh trumpet would point to this being the end and the judgment of the world?